Allegorizings

As I Saw the U.S.A. (1956)

Sultan in Oman (1957)

The Market of Seleukia (1957)

Coronation Everest (1958)

South African Winter (1958)

The Hashemite Kings (1959)

Venice (1960)

Cities (essays; 1963)

The Outriders (political; 1963)

The Presence of Spain (1964)

Oxford (1965)

The Pax Britannica Trilogy (1968–1978)

The Great Port (for the Port of New York Authority; 1969)

Places (essays; 1972)

Conundrum (1974)

Travels (essays; 1976)

The Oxford Book of Oxford (ed.; 1978)

Destinations (essays; 1980)

The Venetian Empire (1980)

The Small Oxford Book of Wales (ed.; 1982)

A Venetian Bestiary (1982)

The Spectacle of Empire (1982)

Wales, The First Place (with Paul Wakefield; 1982)

Stones of Empire (with Simon Winchester; 1983)

The Matter of Wales (1984)

Journeys (essays; 1984)

Among the Cities (essays; 1985)

Last Letters from Hav (novel; 1985)

Scotland, The Place of Visions (with Paul Wakefield; 1986)

Manhattan '45 (1987)

Hong Kong (1988)

Pleasures of a Tangled Life (1989)

Ireland, Your Only Place (with Paul Wakefield; 1990)

Sydney (1992)

O Canada! (essays; 1992)

Locations (essays; 1992)

Travels with Virginia Woolf (ed.; 1993)

A Machynlleth Triad (with Twm Morys; 1994)

Fisher's Face (1995)

Fifty Years of Europe (1997)

Lincoln (1999)

Our First Leader (Welsh fantasy, with Twm Morris; 2000)

Trieste and the Meaning of Nowhere (2001)

The World (2003)

Contact! A Book of Encounters (2010)

Ciao, Carpaccio? (2014)

Battleship Yamato (2018)

In My Mind's Eye (2019)

Thinking Again (2020)

Allegorizings

Jan Morris

LIVERIGHT PUBLISHING CORPORATION

A division of W. W. Norton & Company

New York · *London*

For information about permission to reproduce selections from this book,
write to Permissions, Liveright Publishing Corporation, a division of
W. W. Norton & Company, Inc., 500 Fifth Avenue, New York, NY 10110

For information about special discounts for bulk purchases,
please contact W. W. Norton Special Sales at
specialsales@wwnorton.com or 800-233-4830

Manufacturing by Sheridan
Book design by Chris Welch
Production manager: Anna Oler

ISBN 978-0-87140-414-5

Liveright Publishing Corporation
500 Fifth Avenue, New York, N.Y. 10110
www.wwnorton.com

W. W. Norton & Company Ltd.
15 Carlisle Street, London W1D 3BS

1 2 3 4 5 6 7 8 9 0

This book is dedicated in love and amusement to

Y MORYSIAD

My life's friend
ELIZABETH

Our children
MARK, HENRY, SUKI, TWM *and* VIRGINIA

Our grandchildren
ANGHARAD, BEGW, DYDDG, GWION, JESS, MEILYR,
RUBEN, SAM *and* TUDWAL

also IBSEN *the Norsk Skogkatt*

Contents

Two

Three

Four

Five

Editor's Foreword

OUR INITIAL CONVERSATION began, coincidentally, on February 14, 2001. It was a fortuitous date, and its significance in retrospect would have pleased Jan Morris—although she would have no doubt frowned upon how commercialized Valentine's Day had become in the United States, a country with which she seemed to have a love-hate relationship that endured to the very end of her life.

"Dear Mr. Weil, I wonder if you remember me," she began coyly. "I was reminded of you the other day because I was approached . . . about the idea of publishing a collection of my travel writing, and I remembered your own kind suggestion four or five years ago of a Selected Works (or something rather less grand!). I can't remember what happened to the notion, but as I have now delivered . . . my final book, to be published in October on my 75th birthday, this might be a less impertinent moment than most to ask if by any chance you're still interested, though in a new incarnation," she wrote.

And with whimsical understatement, she added, "Probably not, but perhaps you'd be kind enough to drop me an e-mail anyway. I hope you're having fun in the 3rd Millennium," then concluded with "All best from Wales and from JAN MORRIS," the intentional capitalization of her name perhaps a reflection of her concern that I might no longer know who she was.

As it turned out, I had approached Ms. Morris in the past, not just once but at least once annually, inquiring at the office of her then–literary agent, A. P. Watt, on my annual buying trip to London. Worried that this was not enough, I also wrote to her at home in Wales, as those were the days when emails were just starting to revolutionize the world and Morris somehow did not seem like the kind of person who favored electronic communication. If I heard back at all, it was always a polite decline from her agent. By 2001, though, she suddenly seemed keen to establish a relationship. In fact, as I would later learn, she had even called my previous employer, St. Martin's Press, which I had departed in 1998, so determined was she to track me down.

The notion that I might not remember her was, of course, preposterous. I had already discovered Jan's books while still a teenager. Inexplicably attuned to good writing style when I was in high school, I had been magnetized by the melodious rhythms of her language. Although this was around the time when she came out with the autobiographical *Conundrum*, about her gender reassignment, I suppose I was that rare reader who was as much transfixed by the prose as by the contents. Honestly, I would study her writing sentence by sentence, and in doing so was mesmerized by the brilliance of her imagery and her seemingly effortless ability to interweave human history into her "reportage," a word that feels inadequate to describe her essays that appeared in various magazines, especially *Rolling Stone*.

It is not surprising, then, that I immediately responded to her Valentine's Day entreaty—yet I recall feeling especially nervous, worried about how my own prosaic language might sound to the master, whose writing had beguiled me numberless times. Perhaps I should try to ventriloquize her written voice? I quickly realized that this thought was as absurd as my trying to climb Mt. Everest, a feat that she had accomplished and reported on as a young man in 1953. I then brought her one-paragraph email to my editorial board and was told that Morris would have to write up a proposal for, as she called it, "A Book About the Late 20th-Century World," an anthology that would combine her finest travel pieces into a geographic portrait of the world she had visited.

With characteristic alacrity, Jan put together a few pages and an outline a few days later. "During the second half of the 20th century I travelled almost constantly around the world, first as a reporter, then as an independent writer of books and essays," she began. "I think it could be claimed that during that period I wrote about more places than anyone else, and I was in a position to witness, and to reflect in my writing, many of the great historical events of the time," among which she listed the first ascent of Mt. Everest, the 1956 Sinai War, the Eichmann Trial in Jerusalem, the South African Treason Trial (involving Nelson Mandela), the construction—and later, destruction—of the Berlin Wall, and the British handover of Hong Kong to China. "As I experienced all this first as a man, then as a woman, it might also be said (although I wouldn't want to make much of this) that my viewpoint was unique," she noted while emphasizing that this was not to be a new autobiography.

Presenting her outline to my colleagues, I said that *The World: Life and Travel 1950–2000*, as she chose to call it, would become a retrospective portrait of the late twentieth-century world that would be, as Jan put it, "filtered of course through my own particular vision," since she was "more concerned with the feel of it than with what happened to it." Her emphasis on style and sensibility pleased me greatly, as it did my editorial board. I was approved to offer a modest advance, which she and her agents immediately accepted, the result being our first collaboration.

The notion, however, that this would be her last book turned out to be preposterous. Nothing could prevent Jan from returning to the proverbial inkwell, and although the volumes became slenderer, there would be five additional books that we would publish over a period of nearly two full decades—and that's not including *Allegorizings*.

You can appreciate my surprise when Jan confided to me one day in 2007 that she was writing a "posthumous book," one that could only be published after her death, which she hoped would not be for many years. It was not, she emphasized, the sort that contained salacious revelations—nothing like, say, E. M. Forster's posthumous autobiographical novel, *Maurice*. It may be an understatement to say that this was one of the strangest requests in my forty-year editing career, which now extends to well over 750 books. But after a contract was signed for *Allegorizings*, we went through several rounds of edits, followed by another round of copyediting, after which Jan reviewed both the copyedited manuscript and the first-pass galley pages, and then approved the book design and the jacket itself.

Upon one of her numerous visits to New York—in which she typically wore a slacks or a pair of blue jeans; a bulky, off-white sweater; and an obligatory string of pearls (which I suspected were not real, as I knew that Jan had virtually no interest in jewelry or the international vagaries of fashion)—she eagerly agreed to take part in an interview about *Allegorizings*, the proviso being that its contents could only be released upon publication. The interview, arranged by my colleagues Louise Brockett and Steve Colca, took place in our chairman's office. Unfortunately, because of time considerations, we were unable to go to lunch at the fabled Four Seasons Restaurant, whose soaring modernist architecture appealed to Morris. A meal there could easily become a three-hour Lucullan event, one in which the owners, the chefs, and old-time waiters would dutifully queue up to greet Jan at her regular corner table in the Pool Room. They were, of course, grateful for the many times she had written about the establishment, but it was evident from their joy and the pile of lagniappes on our table that they regarded her as a beloved member of the Four Seasons family.

While an air of joviality characterized all our meetings—evident as well in all of Jan's encounters with waiters, desk clerks, office receptionists, bellhops, and regular folks on the streets of Manhattan—she turned more pensive and reflective during this "posthumous interview." It quickly became clear that Jan was hardly unaware of the challenges and hardships that had shaped her life, be it her struggle with her gender or the death of her beloved daughter, yet she quipped right at the beginning of the interview that "one of the advantages of writing a posthumous

book is that you're never going to have to read the reviews."
She observed that she had "been contemplating death for a long
time," adding, "Don't we all?" For more than thirty years, she
noted, she had kept a carved gravestone under the stairs of her
house, inscribed with these words: "Here are two friends, Jan
and Elizabeth Morris, at the end of one life"—the implication
being that she and her life partner "were so close that we live
one life anyway."

The posthumous book that had initially begun as a series of
letters to a child she and Elizabeth had lost was scrapped as too
"pompous." "It wasn't entertaining, it was somber and gloomy,"
so she felt she had to do "something totally different," a book
that would have to "express it all between the lines, so to speak."
Aware that *Allegorizings* contained no "hideous secrets," Jan felt
nonetheless that "it's a very intimate book, it's the most personal
book I have ever written . . . and it contains aspects of myself that
I don't particularly want to share among my contemporaries . . .
no revelations in it at all . . . except if you read between the lines."

Claiming that she had "been a superficial writer really . . .
a flibbertigibbet kind of writer," Jan commented that she had
"had a great life" and that she had "gotten through life enjoying
herself very much." But in the case of her posthumous work,
it was important to emphasize allegory because the "one thing
about allegory is that often—if you explore it—you'll find on the
other side of almost any substance an altogether different kind of
substance," for if you "have turned the plate around a bit . . . you
see more of what is behind and less of what's in front." Yet despite
the theme of allegory, Jan maintained that the book's chief message was to "keep smiling," and that it was "a hopeful book in a
way," one in which she intended to show that "merriment comes

through as a matter of fact in most situations in life," that "if you keep smiling, you'll get through to the other side."

Alas, Jan did not die as she hoped she would. She had expressed a wish to "take a bottle of burgundy on a winter day and go out on one of the mountains around the home and settle down" to drink the contents of the bottle "and perhaps have some music on a record player and freeze to death. And I'd have left notes at home to say exactly where to discover the corpse. That seems a very nice way of exiting," and then she laughed. As to a belief in an afterlife, Morris was downright skeptical: "It's inconceivable to me that these old medieval ideas of crime and punishment and virtue rewarded can conceivably be true. They're perfect nonsense, aren't they," she asked rhetorically, adding "don't believe a word of it. The only way to look at the afterlife is with a sense of wonder and a sense of mystery and a sense of this allegory," posing a philosophical fillip that "maybe we are [already] in the afterlife now."

Over a period of more than an hour, Jan ranged widely on everything from Sir Edmund Hillary's funeral to her regret at not having pursued a career as a novelist to the impossibility of redemption. Never far from her consciousness was the toponymic importance of Wales, a "powerfully centripetal force" in her own life and on "people who have experienced it all." It was her wish that her entire corpus of books be considered her literary legacy, and that her *Pax Britannica* trilogy be remembered as her most substantial work—because, as only Morris could comment, "it concerns a period that is now as dead as a dodo." In retrospect, it was a remarkable observation to make in 2009, more than a decade before Britain's exit from the European Union.

There was one subject, however, heavily reflected in the writing of *Allegorizings* and in other late Morris books, that was never unambiguous: Jan's adamantine belief in the power of kindness to help solve the immense problems of the world. Essentially challenging the Darwinian emphasis on warfare and "survival of the fittest," Jan was certain that we had to usher in a fourth world of people "who believe in kindness as the ultimate virtue." Hardly superficial or Panglossian in her thinking, she maintained that "the urge towards some new sort of humane, less politicized way of running societies is common to nearly all of us." In fact, she believed in the power of old ladies to effect such a movement. "If they are anything like me," they must "realize that when everything else is scarred, what is left is a yearning for goodness and kindness."

And so, the Valentine's Day message to a potential editor that began so innocently twenty years ago became something far more significant and urgent over time, a resounding philosophical statement—from Wales, of course—for all of us to believe in the transformative power of compassion with the knowledge that kindness is "the ultimate virtue."

Robert Weil
HUDSON, NEW YORK
JANUARY 2021

Pre-mortem

LONG YEARS AGO my Elizabeth and I lost a daughter, only a few weeks old and named Virginia. My own grief was soon half-assuaged by the arrival of a substitute, as it were, in the person of her younger sister Suki, merry as a dancing star and a delight to me for ever after.

Still, it remained a sadness for me that I had never got to know Virginia, and in my old age, feeling intimations of mortality, I resolved to write a series of high-minded letters to her, rather in the manner of Lord Chesterfield addressing his son. The more I thought about the project, though, the more sententious it sounded, and the less I doubted my qualifications for writing it. If I had any moral principles to declare, I came to realize, they were extremely simplistic. First, there was the supreme importance of kindness as a universal guide to life, by-passing all the mumbo-jumbo of organized religion: secondly, the conviction that almost nothing is only what it seems—everything, in fact, is allegory. This would have made a short, didactic work, so I abandoned it, and being about to become an octogenarian anyway, told everyone that I was not going to publish any more books. They mostly smiled indulgently, but I meant it. However over the years I went on writing articles and lectures and meditations and travel pieces and miscellaneous essays; and as I advanced further towards senility it seemed to me in retrospect that all this material possessed a sort of crepuscular unity.

If only between the lines, I realized, it was bound together by a vague but pervasive literary usage. I was right in my second moral principle: all that time I had been allegorizing!

SEEING ALLEGORIES IN things, or making allegories of them, has not always been admired. Medieval theologians, for instance, accused heretics of allegorizing Holy Scripture, just as modern scholars upset fundamentalists by seeing most of the Bible as allegory. For that matter allegory itself has its opponents, especially as a literary instrument. The *Oxford Dictionary* defines it dispassionately as "the description of a subject under the guise of some other subject of aptly suggestive resemblance," but it is easy to disguise half knowledge, or muddy thinking, or lack of inspiration, as expressions of allegory. Robert Musil once defined writers with a weakness for the form as people who "suppose everything to mean more than it has any honest claim to mean."

I am one of them. I long ago came to think that my life itself was one long allegory, and the older I get, the more my conviction grows. I did not, however, deliberately foster the device. It just crept up on me. Some of the literary subjects of my later decades have been half allegorical from the start—America, for example, and railway trains. Some are subtly tinged with allegory. Some reveal themselves as allegory as I think about them. Some, I admit, I have supposed to mean more than they have any honest claim to mean, and some are really more analogous than allegorical. But I see now that in almost all of them, allegory in one kind or another, the belief that most things in life possess multiple meanings, has subtly affected my perceptions and broadened my vision. Ortega y Gasset once suggested that we all carry upon our backs, like a curled-up roll of film (he was writing in pre-digital times), the legacy of our whole lives. My experience has been that, as I entered my eighties, I began to review that long exposure with new interest: and so I came to detect, especially in later years of the film, this preoccupation with the figurative.

And as the taste for allegory grew upon me, so did a conviction about its ultimate importance. Like most of us as we grow old, I have tinkered with theories about the Meaning of Life, religion and all that, and have reached the conclusion that it is all entirely beyond our reach. We cannot, and never can, know the truth about the great imponderables of life and death. The centuries of theological debate have, alas, been wasted time, and it is futile to pretend that religious faith is anything more than useful discipline and consolation, sustained by wishful thinking.

Except . . . Just as Christian scholars explain the Bible and its miracles as being purely metaphorical, and doubtless many pious churchmen similarly rationalize their own beliefs in the unbelievable, so perhaps the whole conundrum of existence, all the mysteries of creation, the Milky Way and the armadillo, art and mathematics, even love and hate, even the loss of a child— perhaps the whole damned caboodle is itself no more than some kind of majestically impenetrable allegory.

ANYWAY, OVER THE years I put this book together. After a peripatetic life I roughly assembled it around a theme of travel; and since it was a book permanently in progress, as it were, to which I would be adding bits, pieces and afterthoughts for the rest of my life, I suggested to my publishers that they might like to publish it posthumously. So it is that, although I am writing this on a sunny spring day in Wales, with lambs outside my window and Elizabeth calling me at this very moment to lunch, by the time you read it I shall be gone!

Jan Morris
TREFAN MORYS
2009

Allegorizings

One

Except perhaps a cat . . .

The Age of Innocence?

PEOPLE OFTEN SAY childhood is the age of innocence. Don't you believe it. There is nobody more cunning, more calculating, often more deceptive, than a human infant (except perhaps a cat, whose most companionable purr can mask a curse . . .) Haven't you seen that evil glare in babies' eyes when, for the fifth time in a row, they throw their rattles out of their prams for the sheer devilish pleasure of making their mothers pick them up? That is the Rattle-Trick, the oldest in the game. Original sin originated in babies, and the seed of malice is innate in them.

I WAS RECENTLY spending an afternoon doing nothing in particular at an outdoor café in the Piazza Unità in Trieste. This is one of the great children's playgrounds of Europe, where they can kick their balls about, push their toy prams, make their first attempts at skate-boarding, all among the memorials and pompous architecture of the city.

Two children particularly interested me that afternoon. One small boy of seven or eight had evidently acquired a new pair of Rollerblades, and was whizzing precariously but ostentatiously around the piazza pursued wherever he went by an adoring younger sister dying to play some part in the adventure. Wherever he whizzed, she tottered after. Whenever he fell over she was there to help. But did he appreciate her loyalty? Did he hell. He only wanted to humiliate her. He was seven or eight years old, and he only wanted to make her feel small. This is called the Squash-Device.

The other child I had an eye on could only just walk, being I suppose less than two years old. He had grown out of the Rattle-Trick technique. He was too young for Squashery. But from every staggering trundle around the square on the hand of an indulgent parent he returned, I noted, with a mordantly calculating look in his eye. Hardly had he settled then in somebody's lap, barely had they taken a sip of their cappuccino, hardly had he accepted a snack of a sweet biscuit or a lump of sugar, than he was wriggling and squirming and fidgeting all over again, depriving his unfortunate parents of their brief and hard-earned moment of relaxation. This was the Walk-Ploy, and with a sigh they succumbed to it every time. All through the long afternoon they walked him, on and off, here and there around the piazza, until the sun began to sink into the Adriatic and it was time at last for little Angelo, kicking and giggling and pushing his baseball cap askew, to be taken victorious off to bed. He had won again. They usually do.

CHILDHOOD, LIKE THE past, is a foreign country. In China it is the sensible practice to lead parties of toddlers through public places tied together with string, and one of the fascinations of Chinese travel is to observe each little face, one after the other, looking up at you with a sweet smile as you pass. Sweet but oddly disturbing, for if you keep an eye on them, you will see that the simper of innocence vanishes instantly when you have passed— to be switched on, like an electric device, by the next child in line. It is as though they are one and all contributors to some collusive subversion—citizens of mischief from somewhere else, rather like goats.

Original sin it may not really be, but original mischief is organic in children (as in goats), and distinguishes them from us. It is their glory and their privilege. The most uncompelling of Christian icons, to my mind, are those that present the Christ-child as a paragon of demure behaviour, looking back at us from the Madonna's lap without a thought of bawling for sustenance from her generous breasts, let alone giving her hair a pudgy tug. A purely divine baby might indeed have no such impulses in his head, but the Christ-child, after all, was human too.

Anyway, you may ask, why am I so conversant with these tricks and ploys of infancy? Because I have helped to bring up five sons and daughters, that's why, and watched the manoeuvres of eight or nine grandchildren. Besides, I was once an infant myself.

In the Midst of Reality

I FOUND MYSELF late one night at a deserted spot ten miles outside Charleston, South Carolina. There a trio of angels, disguised as two sisters and a delightfully loquacious three-year-old called Graham, observed me morosely wondering how on earth I was going to find a taxi into town. Instantly they made room for me in their car and whisked me direct to my hotel. "Thanks for the ride, Graham," said I when we parted. His reply was courteous, but not being fluent myself in three-year-old Carolinian American, for the life of me I couldn't understand a word of it.

When I told a local acquaintance of mine about the angelic intervention, he said: "Oh that's nothing unusual, we're all very nice in Charleston." Actually they weren't always, as I remember too well from my first visit to the place, back in the 1950s heyday of segregation and southern racism, but now it did seem to be true that the most classy of American cities had found, as it were, niceness.

It was a Sunday morning, and its lovely streets were immaculate, its citizens all smiles, its very dogs fastidious, as I made my way to morning service at St. Michael's Episcopalian Church. I should really have gone somewhere more extreme. I should have gone to a Catholic church and been told that it was a sin to vote for a pro-abortion politician. I should have joined an evangelical congregation and had a dose of right-wing fundamentalism. But I chose St. Michael's sure that in that splendid eighteenth-century fane nobody would be very radical either way, and I was right. The service seemed to me a very exhibition of American restraint. There was a minimum of passion of any kind, politics were not mentioned, and the Reverend Richard Belser's sermon was a model parable about marital relationships.

The congregation was discreetly dressed, of course, conversant with the ritual and not at all effusive during the Welcoming. The music was fine, and I was delighted to find tucked into my hymn book the printed programme of a recent wedding at the church, listing in antique italics the names of the seven Groomsmen, the Flower Girl, the two Greeters, the Grandmothers of the Bride, and the Ring Bearer (Howard Wilson Glasgow IV, whose daddy Howard Wilson Glasgow III had been one of the Groomsmen). Could anything be more reassuring?

When we emerged into the sunshine, too, Charleston seemed almost like a propaganda mock-up of an American city. The market brightly bustled, yachts raced off-shore, margaritas evidently flowed, and among the ambling crowds there were not a few inter-racial couples—imagine that, here in the greatest of the slave ports, within sight of Fort Sumter where the Civil War began! It was like a dream. I had an introduction to one of the most beautiful of the seashore houses, currently being restored, and found its owner and her mother awaiting me rather as in a Winslow Homer painting, all sunlit on their balcony above the glistening sea.

They didn't mention politics. They didn't mention the state of the Union. They said how delightful their inter-ethnic workmen were, and told me how skilful and dedicated were the Charleston craftsmen. They weren't in the least surprised to hear about my rescuing angels. They had a blind dog called Chloe. They gave me iced tea, and they sent me away not exactly rejoicing, as the Reverend Mr. Belser might have put it, but decidedly comforted to find this enclave of the ideal in the midst of reality.

Love among the Proverbs

PROVERBS ARE, SO to speak, the catch-phrases of allegory. A favourite of Admiral of the Fleet Lord "Jacky" Fisher, an early twentith-century virtuoso of the catch-phrase, was "The British Navy always travels first class," regularly quoted to himself as he checked into yet another fashionable spa. I was similarly conditioned during my adolescent years as an officer with the Ninth Queen's Royal Lancers of the British Army. At the end of World War II, when we were not getting messy in our dirty old tanks we were making sure that we ate at the best restaurants and stayed at the poshest hotels.

Nowhere did we honour Lord Fisher's proverb more loyally than in Venice, where we happily made the most of our status as members of a victorious occupying army. Many of the best hotels became our officers' clubs, the most expensive restaurants were pleased to accept our vastly inflated currency (which we had very likely acquired by selling cigarettes in the black market). And in particular, since all the motor-boats of the city had been requisitioned by the military, we rode up and down the Grand Canal, under the Rialto Bridge, over to the Lido, like so many lucky young princes.

That was long ago, and I have been back to Venice at least a hundred times since. I have never forgotten Fisher's dictum, and until one day in 2004 I had never once in my life so far neglected it as to take a vaporetto, a public water bus, from the railway station into the centre of the city. There no longer being commandeered motor-boats available, I had invariably summoned one of the comfortably insulated and impeccably varnished water-taxis which, for a notorious fee, would whisk me without hassle to the quayside of my hotel.

My partner Elizabeth had not been subjected to the same influences of adolescence. She spent her wartime years as a rating in the women's naval service, decoding signals in an underground war-room, subsisting on baked beans and vile sweet tea from the canteen. But she had been to Venice with me dozens of times, and I thought that by now I had initiated her into my own Fisherian style of travel. However last time we were there she proved unexpectedly retrogressive. "O Jan," she said as I hastened her towards the line of waiting taxis, ignoring the throbbing vaporetto at its pier, "O Jan why must you always be so extravagant? What's wrong with the vaporetto? Everyone else goes on it. It's a fraction of the price. What's the hurry anyway? What are you proving? We're not made of money, you know. What's the point?"

"The British Navy always—," I began to say, but she interrupted me with a proverb of her own. "Waste not, want not," she primly retorted. Ah well, said I to myself, and to Lord Fisher too, anything for a quiet life: and humping our bags in the gathering dusk, tripping over ourselves, fumbling for the right change, dropping things all over the place, with our tickets between our teeth we stumbled up the gangplank on to the already jam-packed deck.

There we stood for three or four days, edging into eternity, while the vessel pounded its way through the darkness up the Grand Canal, stopping at every available jetty with deafening engine reversals, throwing us about with judderings, clang-ings and bumps, while we stood there cheek by jowl with a ten thousand others on the cold and windy poop. When at last we debouched on the quayside below San Marco, looking as though we were stepping onto Omaha Beach, Elizabeth turned to me with an air of satisfaction. "There you are, you see. That wasn't so bad was it? Think of the money we saved! After all these years, I bet you'll never take one of those exorbitant taxis again. A penny saved is a penny gained."

But she spoke this meaningless maxim too late. Pride, I nearly told her, comes before a fall. Standing there upon the quayside slung about with bags and surrounded by suitcases, I had already discovered that on the vaporetto from the railway station some-body had stolen the wallet that contained all our worldly wealth, not to mention all our credit cards. Off we trudged to the police station to report the loss, and as we sat in the dim light among a melancholy little assembly of unfortunates and ne'er-do-wells, how I regretted ignoring that Fisherism! I bet Elizabeth did, too, although she was too proud to admit it.

I didn't actually say "Penny wise, pound foolish." I did not even murmur under my breath the bit about travelling first class.

Never hit a woman when she's down, I told myself. Virtue is its own reward—and as it happened it was rewarded. We never got that wallet back, but the carabinieri were terribly solicitous, and said how sorry they were, and assured us that no Venetian could have done such a thing—it must have been one of those Albanians—and sent us off feeling perfectly comforted, and a little bit sorry for them, actually, so palpable was their sense of civic shame.

And half an hour later, emotionally drained one way and the other, we turned up on the doorstep of Harry's Bar, a hostelry I have frequented ever since those glory days of victory, when I was young and easy, as the poet said, and Time let me hail and climb. With Jack Fisher metaphorically beside us—he would have loved Harry's Bar—we pushed our way through the revolving door and told our sad story to the people inside.

Lo! they gave us a free dinner (scampi and white wine, with a zabaglioni afterwards) just to cheer us up. For once our proverbs did not conflict. Every cloud, we agreed, as the three of us sat there in the warmth of our first-class corner, really does hide a silver lining.

Transcendental Town

COMPLEXITY, OF COURSE, is an aspect of allegory, which is why whenever I'm in France I try to stop off at Tournus. I like the name of it, for one thing—not one of your pinnacled place-names, but tough and stubby. I like the size of the town, with some 7,300 inhabitants. I like its position on the map, at the bottom end of Burgundy, half-way between Paris and Marseilles. But most of all I like the suggestive complexity of its Frenchness.

On the face of things it has only what one asks of any small French town. It has the Saône River, with the statutory river bridge, pollarded plane trees and idle anglers conventionally catching nothing on its quays. It has an autoroute close by, a celebrated restaurant, a properly pompous Hôtel de Ville, and the double-towered, many-buttressed, austerely arrogant abbey church of St. Philibert. Like so many others in France, the town stands at a junction, where immemorial trade routes converge. The river traffic is mostly pleasure craft nowadays, but often enough a hefty barge churns its way under the bridge, captain's car stowed on its poop, to recall the water commerce of a thousand years. Every morning a majestic swoosh proclaims the passage of the TGV express on its way to Lyon, and along the autoroute, a couple of miles out of town, the trucks and cars swarm as the legions did before them.

But for me the fascination of this place is something more elemental than convergence—more a matter of metamorphosis, in fact. Tournus stands elongated along the west bank of the river, and when I contemplate it from the opposite shore at first it looks straightforward enough. At the top of the town, north of the bridge, the towering mass of the abbey quarter confronts me with its protective turrets, a self-confident enclave which once sheltered all the structures of a powerful Benedictine monastery, and still has a firm, privileged look, with ample villas and gardens down to the river. It is the scene one expects of Burgundy, fit to be embroidered by gentlewomen.

To the left, though, below the bridge, the town unexpectedly runs away down the river-bank in a much less adamant or tapestrian way, and that bold silhouette decays into a fretted jumble of roofs and chimneys, almost anarchic, as though one town, or one culture, has somehow been transformed into another.

THIS SENSATION IS confirmed for me when I cross the river and take a walk through the streets. I start at the abbey quarter, which is indeed remarkably disciplined (except when straggly bus-loads of tourists, or coveys of schoolchildren, are shepherded towards the great church). The shops are craft shops, antique shops, galleries, basket-makers; scholarly-looking men are deep in converse; that famous restaurant is there, and my favourite hotel in all France. I may perhaps hear restrained folk music issuing from upstairs practice-rooms—or even gentlewomen's madrigals?

But south of the abbey, after the bridge, things are soon very different. Now rock music blares from cars at traffic lights. Women shake dusters out of windows. Prickly old codgers mutter to themselves in bars. Cafés abound, and kebab joints. In the middle of the Place Carnot a parked trailer serves crêpes all day long, and on Saturdays the whole length of the town is turned into a serpentine street market, the alleys smell of cheeses, sausages, curry and bunched flowers, and beyond the Hôtel de Ville a couple of costumed Peruvians play funereal Andean harmonies on their pipes.

The very structures seem to me to change, as they themselves meander down the streets. Surely something is happening to the architecture? The skyline grows more raggety, red tiles predominate, glass-enclosed verandas appear, bright blue shutters, external staircases and projecting eaves. A few black people are about now, and Arabs, and like the rooftops, like the colours, little by little as I stroll I feel myself altering too—relaxing, unclenching, perhaps whistling a melody as I walk.

What goes on? The publicists say of the Saône that as it passes through Tournus it surrenders itself to "l'appel du Midi." Now, it seems, I too have crossed some invisible border, and am submitting to the liberating summons of the South.

■

SUCH IS THE piquant, or perhaps picaresque allure that brings
me so often back here. Tournus is a kind of frontier town, but in
the middle of a nation. Here one France kisses another! It seems
to me that upstream from the bridge all is clear-cut and logical,
but below it everything is aesthetically smudged—as though I
have walked out of realism into impressionism. Those civic sentimentalists maintain that when the Saône overflows its banks
here, as it often does, it is not punishing the town but embracing
it: I prefer to think that when the river passes under the bridge
it is celebrating, with a sensuous welling of its waters, just the
complicated frisson that I am feeling too, as I walk out of one
sensibility into another.

Hypochondria

THERE ARE PROS and cons to the equivocal condition of hypochondria. On the one hand it is generally harmless, except perhaps in over-indulgence. On the other hand it is incurable, because there is nothing to cure.

It is really a kind of dreaming. In sleep one has no doubt that a dream is true, and similarly there is no possibility of a mistaken diagnosis of that nagging pain in the back of the hypochondriac's neck—every reference book confirms it, just as every circumstance of a nightmare is utterly convincing.

In a sense both are true. The world of our dreams *exists*, if only in our minds, and a *maladie imaginaire*, though it may not be caused by microbe or decay, is quite genuine enough to its patients. In fact the sufferer may be genuinely rid of it, too, by a placebo—a dream may be consummated by a totally disfunctional orgasm, a non-disease banished by an entirely impotent pill.

Hypochondria certainly has its pleasures. Of course the seduction of self-pity is one, and the morbid fascination of pursuing one's symptoms through the well-thumbed pages of those family medical encyclopedias. I am told that Hemingway habitually took on safari *Black's Medical Dictionary* (probably its tenth edition, 1931), and doubtless spent many a fascinating hour communing with it over his whiskey and his hurricane lamp, while the wild beasts howled.

Like the end of a bad dream, too, a remission from hypochondria can be well worth its discomforts. It is marvellous to wake up, is it not, to discover that we are not after all in the hands of the Gestapo, or still looking desperately for those lost airline tickets; and equally, what a wry delight it is to realize that the stabbing muscular stomach pains of last week could not have been very malignant after all, because they've entirely disappeared this morning!

It is hardly surprising that hypochondria is notoriously a writer's complaint. Writers live by their imaginations, and from Voltaire to James Joyce they have been fascinated by the diseases of fancy. Story-telling is their profession, and as they are often carried away by their own purely fictional characters, so they are all too liable to be infected by epidemics of their minds.

Which means, of course, that for people like me hypochondria is, almost by definition, chronic. Perhaps in extreme old age, when all our powers are fading, we shall lose the requisite imagination. More often, I suppose, the condition deletes itself by turning out to be not imaginary at all, but terminal. Then, if we are anything like Ernest Hemingway, we can put away our Home Medicine for All, pick up a gun and shoot ourselves.

But better still, we can spend our last days recalling our most frightful imaginary illnesses, and contemplating our happy recovery from one and all.

The Traveller

TO A TRAVELLER other people's journeys are not always very interesting, but I was always fascinated by the wanderings of Wilfred Thesiger, the most celebrated explorer of my time, who made his own final journey in 2003, when he was ninety-three years old. I had never been his unequivocal fan, because I scorned his philosophies and thought his life dullened rather than enriched by his vehement rejection of anything modern, but I admired his two great books of travel, *Arabian Sands* and *The Marsh Arabs*, and I marvelled at the courage and dedication that sustained him in so many ghastly journeys in primitive places. He always seemed to me a figurative sort of traveller.

Thesiger concluded very early in life that for him travel was immersion in "colour and savagery," which meant that he denied himself explorations of Europe, the Americas or Australasia, or even parts of Asia and Africa which were insufficiently backward.

"Exploration" in his vocabulary meant the physical discovery of places mostly unknown to outsiders, and the more barren or arid the place, the better the exploration.

He was not, it seems, much interested in the visual arts, he claimed to be tone-deaf, he had no religious conviction and his taste in literature was conservative (like me, as it happens, he particularly liked the poems of James Elroy Flecker). Not for him, then, explorations into the glorious complexities of civilization. It was the clean hard matter of physical challenge that inspired him, and his rejection of all contemporary palliatives took on a semi-mystical character of renunciation.

During the Second World War he was obliged to travel the North African deserts by jeep, but he professed himself unable to change a wheel because he didn't know which way to turn the nut, and he thought the very idea of mechanized desert travel so irrelevant that "had we stumbled upon the legendary oasis of Zarzura, whose discovery had been the dream of every Libyan explorer, I would have felt but little interest." He seemed to think that humanity had reached its apogee in the days before the machine clanked in, and it was in the company of elemental tribal peoples that he found his happiness.

And also, I have to say, his fulfilment. Cynical as I am about his Luddite preferences, I recognize what an artistic unity he made of himself. It may have been distorted by his obdurate dislike of everything new, but within its limits it had true majesty. Thesiger never faltered in his prejudices (except in his willingness to use modern medicine). He believed in them absolutely, and lived and died faithful to them.

HE WAS NOT a handsome man (the writer Gavin Young once said he looked "like a cross between the ultimate Great White Hunter and Widow Twanky"), but from first to last his face looked movingly sad, reproachful and other-worldly—fated, perhaps. Above a great hook nose his eyes look out at us as though they are seeing something else altogether, and his mouth is tightly unsmiling. Even in boyhood it suggests a character impelled, intent upon a single destination, and that not an easy one.

So—speaking for myself—one discovers holiness. It is, I think, an aesthetic spirituality. Thesiger was loyal always to his own ideas of good and evil, simple ideas but genuinely transcendental. He never wavered in his belief that the modern mechanist, materialist ethos was bad, and for most of his life he had nothing to do with it. Almost until the end he lived partly in London, but generally in utmost simplicity in Kenya.

It was the faith of an ascetic, but he attached it to no divinity. One might have thought he would be seduced by the magnificent simplicities of Islam, but he appears to have shown no sign of it: nor did he withdraw into one of his deserts, like the Christian sages of old, to commune with an Almighty. It seems he was an ascetic purely for asceticism's sake, and this conviction in my view attained a sanctity of its own. Thus his long life became something wonderful in itself—a vision, complete and absolute.

I met him only once, shortly before he died. By then he had declined into senility, and seemed only half-aware of the world around him. Perhaps that was a true condition for him. Perhaps all through the years we had been seeing in him a kind of Holy Fool, an instinctive artist in living, with the mind of an innocent and a hero's heart. He would not like this judgement of mine, but then I did not like everything about him, either.

Messages of Bloomsday

THE MOST PROLONGED and affecting of literary allegories concerns the day—June 16, 1904—when Mr. Leopold "Poldy" Bloom spent the day pottering around his native city of Dublin, and bequeathed to the world a celebrated peregrination—so famous that thousands of people still assiduously pursue the route, and June 16 is commemorated to this day as Bloomsday.

Of course Mr. Bloom meandered only through the pages of a novel, James Joyce's *Ulysses*, but that doesn't make his day's wandering any less real to countless aficionados. Whole books have reconstructed Bloomsday Dublin, and Bloom's movements have been timed to the minute. Scholars have noted every shop he passed, every pub he dropped in at, and some of the pubs have prospered by his custom ever since.

It is perfectly possible to accompany Mr Bloom without setting eyes on Dublin—plenty of route maps are available, some even showing the manhole cover, opposite his house in Eccles Street, that he was obliged to avoid at the start of his day, not to mention the direction of the Glasnevin funeral cortège that he joined later in the morning. But there are thousands of readers in the world who feel the urge actually to walk the same pavements, prop themselves at the same bars, and a large proportion of them come to Dublin every June 16.

WHO CALLED IT Bloomsday? The word never appears in the book itself, but as a sort of literary logo it exactly suits the cult that surrounds *Ulysses*. Its knowingess, its in-jokiness, its hint of the T-shirt or the anorak, its commercial potential—all express the nature of this world-wide enthusiasm, which ranges from the academic (e.g., *Ulysses and the Metaphysicals: A Comparative Bibliography*) to the yobbo (e.g., Bloomsday bingeing by the Liffey).

Actually the cult has two epicentres. There is Dublin, of course, of which Joyce himself said his book would be a permanent model, and there is Trieste, where he wrote part of *Ulysses*, and which has a school of Joyce studies and an annual Joyce Symposium. Sometimes the passage of Joyceans between the two cities has a migratory air to it, as the flocks of devotees arrive in their thousands to roost temporarily at one or the other.

The author of *Ulysses and the Metaphysicals* is sure to be there, the man who can recite the whole of Molly Bloom's soliloquy by heart, the couple who fly in every year from Hong Kong, scores of American D.Phil. thesis writers and dozens of earnest addicts, conversant with every last metaphor of the book, who remind me rather of train-spotters. If they are in Trieste they take their coffee-break at the Caffe Stella Polaris, where Joyce was a regular; if they are in Dublin, Davy Byrne's pub is the place. In Dublin the Sandymount Martello Tower, where *Ulysses* opens, compels them one and all; in Trieste they can do the round of the Joyce family's successive uninviting apartments (itineraries obtainable at tourist offices).

Have they all read the book, cover to cover? I very much doubt it. Most people who say they have are evasive when pressed, and all who claim to have read and understood it without a crib are lying through their teeth. Far from being an "accessible" work, as publishers like to claim, much of it is immediately incomprehensible. I myself started to read *Ulysses* in 1942, and I did not succeed in finishing it until 1989, by which time I had acquired Mr. Harry Blamires' indispensable line-by-line commentary, *The New Bloomsday Book*.

For one thing *Ulysses* is, in my opinion, unnecessarily obscure—what's the point? For another it is often tediously ostentatious, in learning as in language. It has so many separate themes, winding and unwinding around one another, that exhausted readers may feel as though they have had one too many at Davy Byrne's—or one too few. And it intermittently purports to be related, episode by episode, to corresponding passages in Homer's *Odyssey*—Bloom himself being its Ulysses, miscellaneous whores and bigots representing Circe, Cyclops, and the rest, and Mrs. Bloom revealing herself, at the very end, as a less than immaculate Penelope.

Joyceans are inclined to be touchy if you mention the opacity of the work, because half their pleasure comes from worrying out the meanings of *Ulysses*, matching texts, arguing about locations and following the Dublin street maps (though Joyce sometimes mischievously confuses even them—now and then he puts a shop on the wrong side of a road, or has somebody getting off a train at Lansdowne Road when the 10 a.m. train from Bray didn't stop there . . .).

AND YET . . . dear God, how often have I blessed Mr. Blamires, ever since he first enabled me to read *Ulysses* all the way through! However maddening this book can be, however boring or pretentious, I recognize it as one of the universal literary masterpieces. There! I have declared myself a Joycean, and as a matter of fact, when I opened one of my several editions of *Ulysses* today, out fell the packaging of a cake of lemon soap, bought years ago at the Sandymount Martello Tower, and sold in memory of the lemon-scented soap that Poldy bought for himself at Sweney's in Lincoln Place (page 69, line 510, 1986 edition). I have kept it for seventeen years, and one can hardly get more Joycean than that.

Actually it was the protean nature of the book that finally convinced me of its greatness. I take nothing back about multithemes and unconvincing Homerisms, and I still feel free to skip whenever I want to. But I marvel now at that tangle of themes which used to tire me so, because it means that the book is, so to speak, many books in one, conveying many parallel messages— and many morals, perhaps.

First and most obviously it is a book about Dublin. Lots of Dublin has disappeared since 1904, but lots hasn't, and it is still a fascination to follow that famous meander through its streets, looking out for the Ormond Hotel where the barmaid-Sirens were, or Nichols the undertakers, or hoping to buy some kidney at Dlugacz's butcher's shop (not a chance, because it is one of the few purely fictional establishments in the book). There we go, we Joycean train-spotters, with our maps in our hands and dear Mr. Blamires in our capacious string bags—year after year, Bloomsday after Bloomsday, deploring still the demise of the Bath Avenue tram, rejoicing to find the coffee fragrant as ever outside Bewley's.

Then *Ulysses* is also the portrait of a man—some critics say the most complete portrait of a man ever written. Bloom is a very ordinary person, except that he is a Jew. He feels an outsider always. He is more sensitive than most ordinary persons, more confused about himself sexually and socially, and as we accompany him around the city, all through the day, we seem to glimpse every last nuance of his character, admirable and pathetic, sad and hopeful.

Ulysses is a study in jealousy, too, because during the afternoon Bloom is cuckolded, and knows it. It is a comedy, sometimes aspiring to farce (but not often, for my tastes, very funny). It is a poem. It is a play. It is a sort of sex manual, because a multitude of sexual preferences and variations are observed, recalled or simply imagined; if Bloom exposes himself in many kinds of pornographic self-indulgence, Molly brings everything to a celebrated climax with eight pages of undiluted and unpunctuated literary orgasm. It is full of sorrows! It has a happy ending!

TO MY MIND the glory of the thing is this: that we can read it how we please (if we manage to read it at all). I choose to find in it an elementary lesson in morality, because I believe that at its core there lies a parable of goodness. "Poldy" Bloom is as fallible a man as ever lived, a lascivious day-dreamer, but he is good at the heart, and my favourite passage in the whole work concerns his passing over O'Connell Bridge at about eleven on Bloomsday morning. As he walks he scrumples up a piece of paper and throws it over the parapet, wondering if the seagulls fluttering around will think it edible. Of course they don't, but a few moments later Poldy feels sorry for those birds, feels ashamed to have tried to deceive them, and buying a couple of Banbury cakes from a nearby stall (price 1d), he crumbles them, returns to the bridge, and makes recompense to the gulls.

One could not be basically bad and do that: and the grand allegorical lesson of *Ulysses* is perhaps that you can be an idler and a lecher, the most pretentious of writers, the most pedantic of scholars, the silliest of literary groupies, the drunkest of louts down at Temple Bar, and still be as kind a man as Leopold Bloom.

A Patron Sinner

A SEMINAL EVENT of the late twentieth century was the death of Princess Diana, killed with her Egyptian lover in a Parisian car accident. It reverberated around the world for decades, so swarming was it with suggestion, innuendo, lascivious gossip, deceit, romance and anomaly—the beautiful English aristocrat, once married to the heir to the throne of England, embroiled in the end with dubious hangers-on and tuft-hunters. Who could have foreseen that a decade later a coroner would still be obliged to deny that her death had been engineered by the British secret service, with the connivance of the Queen of England's husband?

It was a drama with an almost Shakespearian cast. There was the Queen herself, rigidly and honourably obedient to her God-given role as Head of State and Defender of the Faith. There was

her notoriously tactless husband the Duke of Edinburgh, given
to remarks of violent political incorrectness, and popularly supposed to detest his daughter-in-law. There was Diana's divorced
husband Prince Charles, dedicated to organic environmentalism,
and his then mistress Camilla Parker-Bowles, dedicated in particular to horses. There were the two sons of Diana and Charles,
one of them eventually to be King William V, if the kingship
survived that long. There was Diana's lover Dodi Fayed, last in
a line of infatuates, handsome but unmemorable, who was to
die with her in Paris. And there was Diana herself, a burr in the
heart of the monarchy, lovely but sly, devoted to her sons but
notoriously estranged from her husband and his stuffy relatives,
given to insidious interviews with the Press and liable always, so
it seemed, to blurt out some appalling revelation about the royal
institution.

Her funeral was a famous display of kitsch—the entire
English nation, it seemed, once universally celebrated for sang-
froid and stiff upper lip, wallowing in excesses of maudlin emotion. An image of sharing and caring piety had been imposed
upon her by the publicists, and the result was, in my view, that
her memory was honoured in diametrically the wrong way. The
nation mourned a martyr when it should have been celebrating
a miscreant.

For everyone knew that Diana was really no Mother Teresa—
it was doubtless a tacit part of her appeal for the tabloid masses.
She always used to say, though, that she wanted to be an ambassador for her country. People sneered, but they should have taken
her at her word. She should in my opinion have been given the
all-but-superannuated royal yacht *Britannia*, which nobody knew
what to do with, and invited to rollick her way around the world

in the national behalf, living it up without inhibition, taking a new boy-friend to every port (or finding one there), and distributing a taste of outrageous English gaiety among all the nations.

THE WORLD WOULD have adored it. Diana was one of the loveliest women of the age, and left to her own instincts she might have been one of the most entertaining, too—a patrician Elizabeth Taylor, a seagoing Lady Hamilton. Wherever she sailed in her grand old vessel (built in 1953 and now a museum ship in Edinburgh), with its complement of elegant peccadillo sustained by all the splendour of the Royal Navy, she would have caused a cheerful sensation, and the idea of England itself would have been given a much-needed shot of glamour. Did any nation, ever, have a more fascinating envoy at large?

The elderly ship, of course, would have been completely redecorated, and fitted throughout with multi-phonic hi-fi and video equipment. The usual Royal Marine band would have been supplemented by a rock combo, and the crew, headed by a handsome young admiral, personally selected by the Princess with particular emphasis on good looks. The *Britannia*'s appearance would have remained unaltered, except for new and more startling paint colours, but the Royal Barge would have been replaced by a gorgeous Italian-built hydrofoil, together with the speedboats, swimming-pools and hang-gliders necessary to the Princess's purposes.

I like to imagine her arriving at one of the remoter Mediterranean islands—Figesta, let us call it—in the course of her mission (defined by the Lords of Admiralty, in their most august antique prose, as "representing the dignities and furthering the interests of Her Majesty's Kingdom by whatever means and devices She thinks appropriate"). The little port-city is awakened at dawn by the usual reveille gunshot from the Fort of St. Idiama, but this morning it is answered by a deafening 21-gun salute from the harbour. When the smoke clears from the saluting guns the crowds hastening in the half-light down to the waterfront, many of them still in their night-clothes, are astonished to discover in the very centre of the bay, dressed all over, lights blazing from prow to stern and huge standards at every masthead, the pink and gold presence of *Britannia*.

Enormously amplified there then sound from its loud-speakers a recording of "God Save the Queen," but before its last chord has died away, merciful Heaven the rock combo is in full blast, twice as loud, twice as bold, and all around the town, bouncing from fortress walls, echoing from the mountains, bringing every last inhabitant out into the streets, hurrying the *polizie* down to the quay with guns already cocked, summoning the Provincial Governor himself and his portly wife amazed in their dressing-gowns to the balcony of their palace, the thump and squawl of punkism shakes the awakening dawn.

The visit to Figesta is a triumph—one long celebration, almost an orgy, embracing the whole island in an ecstasy of enjoyment. Diana, wearing a summer dress of flaming crimson and an amazing hat, goes ashore attended by the Admiral in full-dress uniform, and strolls merrily about the city streets blowing kisses to men old and young, embracing children, jollying along old ladies, tickling the chins of policemen, sometimes breaking into a few steps of a waltz and showered with flowers from upstairs apartments. Huge crowds follow her, singing and laughing, mock-saluting the Admiral and urging her to come inside, lady, come and have Figesta wine. By midday the whole town is in a condition of happy chaos, and even the stern carabinieri are parading arm in arm like chorus boys.

By the time they reach the Governor's palace His Excellency and his lady are ready for them, and wait in full panoply (epaulettes for him, feathers for her) between the ceremonial stone dolphins at the door. Don Giorgio the elderly Governor falls to his knees, Signora Minelda sinks into a profound curtsey, but the Princess cries "Oh, you silly old things, let's have none of that nonsense," and pulls them both boisterously to their feet. She kisses each of them heartily on their cheeks, she tousles the Governor's hair, she says ooh how smashing is his lady's feather boa, and presently accompanies them into the state dining-room for a buffet luncheon—Diana giggling, the Governor in uncontrollable fits of laughter and Her Excellency already merrily dishevelled.

So it goes, all that day and through the night. There is nonstop dancing in the streets. Wine flows out of every fountain in town, and runs down the very gutters. The band is in full frenzied flow as the evening lights come on, and merrily drunken sailors from the *Britannia* rollick in squares, flirt in courtyards and enthusiastically whistle whenever they glimpse the Princess. At sunset the Governor and his party are taken on board the hydrofoil for a champagne whizz around the harbour before a shipboard dinner, which is extremely convivial, lasts a long time and concludes with a showing of the television show *Dad's Army*, a favourite of the Governor's wife.

"It *has* been fun," Diana tells them as the gubernatorial party is piped ashore, the Admiral saluting and half a dozen hastily sobered ratings standing at attention. "Thank you *so* much—oops, mind how you go, Minelda dear—goodnight, Giorgio—lovely to have met you, and all your darling people—what a smashing place you have here! *Buoa noche*—is that how you say it? Mind how you go! Have fun!" And a few hours later, when the sun comes up, the people of Figesta emerge sleepily into the streets, and Giorgio and Minelda look wistfully out to sea from their balcony, *Britannia* has gone.

Could the Queen's worst enemies have resisted such diplomacy?

THE ENGLISH TRIED to make Diana a patron saint, but she was much better suited to be a patron sinner. She was not a serene young novitiate at the altar rail, she was more a mixed-up kid, as they used to say in her time, a kid next door, in trainers and a baseball cap out on the town.

The mass British public adored Diana as it adored rock stars or footballers, with a hysteria that was stoked constantly by the tabloid Press, and she was presented as the very antithesis of everything that the British Crown represented, with its age-old traditions of pomp, protocol and imperial complacency. No matter that she was herself an aristocrat, from one of England's oldest families. She was thought of as a young confessor to unmarried mothers, divorcees, night-clubbers, rockers and rebels everywhere. She consorted with showbiz celebrities. She was the epitome of populist glamour. Moreover, patrician though she was, there was something reassuringly *common* about her. She was less like the descendant of an ancient earldom than like the expensively educated though not very bright eldest daughter of a self-made billionaire. Undeniably beautiful though she was, she was better suited to a Dodi Fayed than to a Plantaganet.

St. Teresa of Avila is cherished because she often lost her temper with God. Churchill is beloved although he was a boozer and a reactionary, Nelson although he was an adulterer. Diana should be remembered not as a victim or a martyr, as her ageing fans remember her, but as a national emblem of risk and delight. Too late! Having dined at the Ritz that summer night in 1988, the poor girl died with her playboy in the back of a Mercedes limousine—far too soon, but not an unsuitable end for her. They should have given her *Britannia* while the going was good, and she might still be roaming the ocean waves with Dodi or another, refuelled by tankers at sea and admirers on shore, and taking with her something of Merrie England—remember Merrie England? —wherever she disembarked.

T w o

Three ships came sailing

Ships of Youth

THREE SHIPS REPEATEDLY came sailing into the imagination of my youth. I spent much of my adolescence in their figurative company, and sixty years on I look back to them as to kinds, or aspects, or exemplars of youth itself. Others may see youth personified in three graces: for me it is in three great ships.

It was the age of the great ships, and in particular of the North Atlantic liners, before long to be as extinct as the galleon or the clipper ship. I grew up in the knowledge and the fascination of them, and especially of three iconic vessels whose construction and celebrity spanned the years of my own youth. One was French, one British, one American, and for me to this day they each express one attribute of that marvellous condition, being young.

The youngest was the French *Normandie*, which was launched

at San Nazaire, in a frenzy of patriotic pride, when I was six years old. Next came the *Queen Mary*, whose construction on the Clyde sent the British Press almost into hysterics when I was ten. A third was the *United States*, built and launched with less fanfare at Newport News in my twenty-fifth year. The lives of the three vessels overlapped, which meant that they were present in my consciousness for nineteen years of my susceptible youth.

Contemplating them now, in my memory as in my fancy, really is like analyzing my own salad years, because in each of them I see some facet of what I wanted to be like myself. Great ships exert their personalities just as humans do. I always remember the Cunard official who remarked to me once of the new *Mauretania* (built 1939) that her two funnels were too close together—not because they produced insufficient draft, or added too much top-weight to the vessel, but because they were "out of character." The thing about my three ships was this: that each one was a complete personality, balanced in itself, and self-sufficient, with smokestacks where they should be.

I WOULD BE deluding myself if I claimed to see much of my own nascent personality in the *Normandie* (79,300 tons). She is often said to have been the most beautiful liner ever built, and she was made for adulation. Never since the days of the China clippers, perhaps, was a ship fashioned with such grace and instant fascination. Just the look of her was her own logo, and one of the most famous poster pictures ever was the stunning bow view of the *Normandie* painted by Cassandre in 1935—her vast stylized bulk filling the printed page, perfectly immaculate, with a tiny tricolour at her prow and sprinkled gaily across the shadowy side of her hull, a little flock of thirteen white sea birds, frolicking in her flank.

The picture speaks of power, modernity, calm (for only the merest flicker of a bow wave shows), and pleasure—pleasure especially, because it is those cavorting gulls that steal the scene. The *Normandie* was certainly the most exhilarating of my three ships, attuned to celebrity from the start, and she was decorated in such a riotous excess of art deco, such an avant-garde extravagance of paintings, tapestries, carpets, etched-glass windows—adorned with so many ornamental columns, symbolical murals and statues—stocked with such splendid wines and mouth-watering victuals—frequented by such marvellously dressed aristocrats, artists, actors and ladies of fashion—sailing the seas, in short, in such almost unapproachable sophistication that if we are to believe the publicity pictures it was all a trifle vulgar.

But gloriously, sensuously vulgar. Somebody gave me a cutaway picture of the *Normandie*, which opened into three sheets displaying the vessel in full glory, and I used to love peering into its cabins and staterooms, the vast Grand Salon full of black-tied gents and befurred ladies, the smoking-room approached by a flight of stairs fit for any presidential entrance, the concert hall where I imagined Louis Armstrong and Josephine Baker in full blast as the ship sailed on.

Some of all this I envied, and half-wished that it represented my kind of world: but at other times I viewed it with a scornful eye, and thought that ship of magnificent hedonism—the largest, and fastest, and most powerful of its day—unworthy of its calling.

FOR IF I wasn't exactly a prig, I was a wartime foundling, and I chiefly admired qualities of strength, perseverance, even austerity—the qualities most cherished in Churchill's Britain. The next ship that came sailing into my mental seas was, in those respects at least, more to my taste. The *Queen Mary* (80,300 tons) was, as it happens, bigger and faster than the *Normandie*, but she was not half so glamorous. Completed in 1936, and hailed by the British with just as much hyperbole as the French had greeted the *Normandie*, she had in truth not much about her that was novel. She stood recognizably in the line of the famous Cunarders of the past, like the ancient *Aquitania*, which was still in service then, and her personality was inherited—when that Cunard man complained to me about the *Mauretania*'s funnels, he was thinking of the corporate style of his company, which indeed reached a climax in the huge three-funneled *Queen Mary*.

She was a bit boring, actually—big, strong, fast, grand, but rather dull. She had none of the innate charisma of the French ship, but she truly represented the capital virtues of the British. Not very excitingly modernist, her decor was replete with imperial referrences—every British colonial possession seemed to have contributed some native wood carving or indigenous craft. Of course, portraits of the eponymous monarch abounded (although legend says that the Cunard Line originally intended to call the ship the *Queen Victoria*).

But there, the Queen Mary fitted her times, her nation, and her heritage, and I was vicariously proud of her. She represented in my mind the ethos of the stiff upper lip, and I was big on that in those days.

I ALSO ADMIRED the reckless, the dashing, the incorrigible, and no ship ever satisfied those philosophical criteria better than the *United States* (53,350 tons), which erupted into the Atlantic after World War II, when I was in my twenties. She was a secret ship, and that intensified her allure for me.

Secret, because she was really not a proper passenger ship, but a quasi ship of war, and I admired the martial virtues, too. She was intended always to serve when needed as a kind of super-troop-ship, and for years the details of her hull were not released to the public. Her speed was kept secret into the late 1970s, although she had long proved herself the fastest liner on the Atlantic.

The look of her, anyway, was exciting enough. Not as thrilling as the *Normandie*, not as impressive as the *Queen Mary*, something about her stance, I thought, spoke of raffishness, slinkiness, perhaps a little criminality. There was nothing wooden about her—literally, for her visionary designer William Gibbs insisted that everything must be of metal—partly as a precaution against fire, partly to reduce weight and increase speed. So the whole ship, in substance and in style, was metallic. Two enormous oval funnels were placed well forward, giving the vessel a suggestion of powerful impetus, and on board the ship, with steel corridors and metal fittings everywhere, and lashings of aluminium, there was no pretending that you were anywhere but on board a seagoing mechanism. Nobody was going to say, on the *United States*, what a small boy said to his mother when she took him for the first time down the gilded elevator to the *Normandie*'s voluptuously glittering Grand Salon, "But Maman, when are we going to see the *ship*?"

So the *United States* was the third of my ships, and I rejoiced with her when, many years later, I read that her maximum speed had been released to the public at last: 44 knots, faster than any other passenger ship ever built. I envied her characteristics, too. I wanted to be lean, fast and raffish, like her.

THUS I COVETED the qualities of all three, an admission Freud might have relished—rather more interesting perhaps, than the old urges to murder one's father, or be a fish. I wanted to be elegant, I wanted to be strong, I wanted to be racy, and so I transported myself in fancy, during the later decades of my adolescence, to one or another of my three Atlantic liners.

They responded in kind. The fabulous *Normandie* spent her last years ignominiously sitting out the war at New York's Pier 88, until she was burnt out and broken up. The *Queen Mary* behaved as you would expect of her, transporting hundreds of thousands of soldiers across the Atlantic, braving the worst the U-boats could threaten: and she is with us still, like a dowager in reduced circumstances, keeping a stiff upper lip as a floating museum in Long Beach, California. As I write the *United States* is still afloat too, gutted and emasculated at Philadelphia as a potential cruise ship: but her speed records have never been beaten, and when I want to, I can still re-create in my mind the bold metallic vibrations of my tourist-class cabin, when she whisked me home across the Atlantic at the start of my maturity.

Us against Them

LONG AGO IN Wales in the days of beads and Beatles, I marvelled to hear that a village on the coast of northern California had communally opted out of the world. Its name was Bolinas. Its citizens had removed their road signs, to dissuade uninvited and unsuitable visitors, and they had defiantly declared a kind of New Age separatism.

Of course many people scoffed—those crazy Californians!—but for me that small item of news, on the inside pages of the newspapers, was like a little flame flickering in the west. It signified individuality challenging conformity, eccentricity cocking a snook at normality, Us defying Them, small against big.

NOT THAT THERE then seemed to me much wrong about the bigness of the United States. Whenever I visited the country I was captivated, like almost all visitors, by the majestic scale of it—by the mighty landscapes of course, but no less by the colossal energy and confidence of the place. I loved the great trains criss-crossing the continent, and the airports with their myriad flights arriving from the four corners of the Republic, and the burgeoning skyscraper cities, and the roster of exotic names—Duluth and Albuquerque, Milwaukee and Miami and Chattanooga. . . . I loved the speed of everything, I loved the swaggering generosity, and although there were often times when I disliked American policies, I thought it marvellous that on the whole this gigantic power seemed to exert its bigness for the good of humanity. In those days most of humanity thought the same.

All the more wonderful, I thought, that in such a society, at such a time of history, the people of Bolinas had exhibited their inalienable right to pursue happiness in their own way, totally disregarding all the conventions, and some of the values, of their own overwhelmingly persuasive society. What did they call themselves—hippies, beats, flower people? I forget, but next time I was in California I found my way to Bolinas, and discovered that it was everything I had imagined it to be.

Sure enough, no road sign guided me there, and in the tumbledown little village the whole uproarious repertoire of 1970s radical America greeted me. It was all there—the idealism and the nonsense, the mystic cults, the pony-tails and the junkies, organic turnips and aromatherapy, bold feminism, socialist slogans, strumming Dylanesque guitars, all enveloped within what was, for my tastes, an exhilarating sense of live and let live.

It seemed to me an admirably idiosyncratic enclave, there on the edge of the superpower, and when I returned to more ordinary demonstrations of the American Way, I did not feel that

Bolinas stood in opposition to their ideals, but was only quite properly contributing a stitch or two to the most endearing of historical quilts.

THIRTY YEARS ON, in the next century, I went to Bolinas again. When I drove up Highway 1 from San Francisco—past the redwood groves, past the strand where the seals and the pelicans sunned themselves—even then there was nothing to tell me where the turn-off was. And when, more by instinct than memory, I found my way once more into the hugger-mugger hamlet, I discovered that the beats, the aquarians, the children of the summer of love, the psychedelians or whatever they used to call themselves were still in residence.

Nowhere is immune to the world's corrosions, but if there is one small place where the ideas of those visionary, hallucinatory generations poignantly survive, it must surely be Bolinas, California. In the very centre of the place I found a Spirit House, a shrine which was erected only in 2000 to provide a focal point for the community. A few bikes were propped against it, some votive gourds and vegetables were disposed here and there, and the central effigy of glass and concrete, yearning skyward aspirationally, was identified as Spirit in the Physical Realm.

Not many communities of the Western world, in our dawning Age of Uncertainty, would erect a public focus so unabashedly mystic. It is true that in the real estate agents' window across the way the cheapest of the five houses on offer was $537,000, and the most expensive over $4,000,000, but a featured band at Smiley's Schooner Saloon that week was named Huckklebuck and the

What You Wants, and outside the saloon, in the middle of the morning when I drove in, a bearded man with an accordion was singing a not very politically correct folk song (Oooo! I don't want her, You can have her, She's too fat for me . . .).

Around the corner was the People's Coop Grocery, the most absolutely green, most ineluctably toxic-free grocery store on earth, and next door there was a sort of exchange shack, where people could pick up a free T-shirt or a paperback, and drop off some rubbish of their own. On the door of a pick-up the word PEACE was spelled out in glued sea shells; in a shop window business hours were defined as "1-ish to 5-ish."

A few ageing drop-outs were hunched over the day's papers at the Coast Cafe, sporadically grunting or exclaiming incredulously to people at neighbouring tables "D'ya see what these ass-holes are saying now?" Some of them were probably distinguished novelists (several had settled in Bolinas, over the years), others looked to me like elderly junkies or lay-abouts, but their coexistence was evidently amiable. On a nearby notice-board, I was comforted to observe, somebody was offering Humane Animal Removal of Skunks, Etc, and in the Bolinas *Hearsay News* I read that somebody else had FOUND a "very emaciated, tawny, hungry, sick, maybe old, friendly and unfrightened Cat. . . ."

SO I FELT *comforted* by Bolinas? Well, in a way I did. I was comforted that the Skunks would be humanely Removed, and that the Cat was unfrightened. I was glad to see that Huckklebuck and his mates were prospering.

For the America that I was travelling through had changed

its character in thirty years. It remained the biggest of all the nations, and in my judgement still in many ways the best, but it had somehow lost its grandeur. To the world at large it no longer represented all that was hopeful and generous in human affairs; to itself, I felt, it presented an uncertain image. Gone was that wonderfully seductive confidence, gone the certainty that what was good for America was good for mankind. The endearing youthful swagger had become a paunchy strut. Hubris was in the air too, and with it a touch of unwitting pathos, for by definition hubris portends humiliation.

So yes, it was a sort of comfort to find that in Bolinas, the funky little outpost of old American liberties that had excited me long ago, where Jefferson might well have felt at home, if perhaps not George Washington—in Bolinas, California, the style of things was recognizably still the same. The old flame burnt less brightly, mind you. Thirty years ago Bolinas was a vivid, preposterous sort of place. Now it is just a place without a road sign, where yesterday's idealisms potter quietly on, deprived of their wayward brilliance.

Once, to a European like me, its name evoked the spirit of a grand idea, a truly American idea, away in the distant west. Today it too is hazily groping, like the Great Republic itself, like the rest of us around the globe, towards some ever more evasive truth—towards the Spirit in the Physical Realm, perhaps, or perhaps even now, as a sadly nostalgic flyer outside the Bolinas village store suggested to me, towards "the Sacred World of Shamanic Mushroom Rituals."

Ah yes, remember the mushroom rituals?

The Furrier

ONE OF MY favourite people in life was Joseph Gluckstein Links, the London-born son of a Hungarian refugee. He was J. G. Links of Calman Links, the furriers, and he himself was actually the Royal Furrier.

He was by no means *just* a furrier, though, and not being a great supporter of the fur trade, I got to know him through other channels altogether. When in 1960 I published a book about Venice, the very first letter I got about it was from J. G. Links. I had never heard of him, and he introduced himself simply as a fellow aficionado of the city. It turned out that he was much more than that. He was perhaps the greatest living authority on the Venetian painter Canaletto, and he probably knew Venice as well as any foreigner alive.

But Joe Links was much more than that, too. He was an expert on German wines. He wrote books about Ruskin and about townscape painting. He devised a number of best-selling detective stories, with the crime writer Dennis Wheatley, which were really dossiers, including between their pages physical clues, like blood-stained handkerchiefs, or Scotland Yard fingerprints. The reader was never actually told who the murderer was—if you were terminally baffled you'd find the solution in a sealed envelope at the back. The books were a vast success around the world, except in Nazi Germany, where the censors forbade them—the moral values of these books, they decreed, "must be designated more than inferior, created for English living conditions, not German ones." (Also, of course, Joe was a Jew . . .)

He had spent World War II in the RAF, on some secret work, I have always supposed. He loved boats and fast cars, and before the war he was a regular on the Cresta Run at St. Moritz. But he was anything but flashy himself. It is true that he liked to live well. In Venice he always stayed at the Danieli Hotel—twice a year in most years, and when I once asked him why he didn't buy a house there, he said what was the point of *buying* a house when you could *stay* in a house with 120 attentive servants. But he was a quite particularly modest, unassertive man, slight and stocky, quietly debonair, and he was at his very best when he was at home.

He had married Mary Lutyens, a daughter of Lutyens the architect and a distinguished writer herself, and they lived together in devoted harmony for more than fifty years. I loved to visit them at their home in London. They lived in a building overlooking Hyde Park. Their rooms were on the top floor, and they had their library in the basement, so that if Joe wanted to look something up in a book he had to take the lift down to find it.

In all other respects they lived in enviable comfort. Joe would welcome me at the door wearing, as often as not, an exotic caftan, and Mary would be reclining in an armchair with a martini, stirred I would think rather than shaken, and Joe would listen to my not very interesting news with the most intense interest, hanging on my every word as though he were memorizing it all for an exam, and sometimes gently, almost increduously interrupting to say something like, "You really mean you had to have the *plumber* in?"—as if our petty domestic problems were of unsurpassable interest to him.

HIS HAPPIEST PUBLIC memorial will probably be his book *Venice for Pleasure*. This has been in print for years and years, and it has given his relationship with the city a unique charm. His was a profound and guileless love of the place, and none of Venice's innumerable chroniclers have portrayed the Serenissima's character with quite such a combination of the scholarly, the informal and the intimate.

You might think his attitude to Venice innocent, and in a way it was, because his book is not only called *Venice for Pleasure*; it really is a sort of pleasure manual, too. Its author describes himself as "the perennial tourist," travelling purely for enjoyment, but it would be misleading to think of it merely as a work of hedonism. Joe Links was of course an allegorical man, masking his extreme sophistication in apparent simplicity. Over the years thousands of readers, starting to read his book, have been relieved to encounter its famously undemanding approach to the city—"Generally the first thing to do in Venice is to sit down and have some coffee"—but by the time they get to the end of it, all the same, they will have learnt virtually everything that an educated stranger needs to know about the place, its art and its history, besides being subtly entertained throughout.

It has happened almost without their realizing it, for the Links literary style is at once deceptive and essentially *considerate*. He is the very opposite of those noisy tour guides we are sure to pass, brandishing their placards, as we follow his easy prose through the streets. He never pushes us, never bullies, never shows off, never condescends. We don't *have* to be interested in fourteenth-century mosaics, and *Venice for Pleasure* is surely the only guidebook—if "guidebook" is the word for it—that occasionally confesses itself surfeited with wonders, or bored in a gallery of art.

"If all the circumstances are propitious," Joe says almost at the end of his book, "I can promise you the most delightful experience that even Venice has to offer." He is talking about an out-of-season dinner at the Locanda Cipriani on the island of Torcello, and we can be sure that his own pleasure is tinged by the memory of some lovely evening of his own, long ago perhaps: but it is enriched, as well, by all the delights of Venice through which he has been guiding us since page one—delights sensual very often, but delights of the intellect, too, enhanced by his humour, and by the deep knowledge of history and art that he has been unobtrusively sharing with us.

HE WAS A wonder. You would never for a moment guess that he knew all that there was to know about the fur trade, about Canaletto, about Rhine wines, about the Cresta Run, about heaps of other things he hardly ever mentioned. He was as kind, merry, and generous a person as you could ever hope to meet. His last triumph was the great Canaletto exhibition he organized for the Metropolitan Museum in New York, and by then he was eighty-five years old. When he died, in 1997, his widow said simply of him, "Joe was everything a man should be," and how could one disagree?

Style in Adversity

SOPHISTICATION THAT LOOKS like simplicity is my own idea of style, and one of its epitomes, to my mind, is a small hotel I know in rural France. It is remote, and not conventionally luxurious. Beringed tycoons might not think much of it, but as its proprietress once reminded me, dukes frequent it.

Style shows at its best in adversity, and once I had occasion to see this little hostelry at its most imperturbable. A great storm had swept France, and when we came to check out, the electric power was off and none of the credit card mechanisms were working. We had no hard cash. We had no travellers' cheques. We had a train to catch. What to do?

The whole hotel staff, it seemed to me, assembled to deal with this crisis. There was the magnificent Senegalese lady receptionist. There were two or three Arab-looking maids. There was the curly-haired hotel terrier, and two refugee kittens loudly squalling in a nearby basket. On his knees on the floor was a young electrician, contemplating his fuses in a scholarly way, and sometimes a gently smiling middle-aged Frenchman drifted through with a watering-can. Now and then there sounded from somewhere out of sight the calmly authoritative voice of Madame La Patronne.

We had four different credit cards between us, and we tried them all. None of them worked. We tried them back to front, inside out, we rubbed them on our skirts. The electrician on the floor took no notice at all as we swapped one card for another, but once Madame's contralto offered comforting but totally ineffectual off-stage advice.

Back came the man with the watering-can, the Arab girls crowded around the reception desk, the electrician hummed to himself, a woman in a bikini turned up to clean the windows, and suddenly there was a bleeping noise from a credit card machine. The receptionist seized one of our cards and jammed it in, and miracle! the machine responded. Limp with relief, we watched as it began to churn out its paper. It was like the resolution of a fugue.

But no, it was better than that. It was the development of a farce, because whatever any of us did then, whatever buttons we pressed, inexorably that paper kept on coming out. It spilled all over the table, it curled all over the floor, and by the time I managed to grab it in passing and sign my name on it, we were all helpless with laughter, and the splendid Senegalese had collapsed hilariously shaking into an armchair.

Presently Madame emerged into the chaos from her Olympus. "It has been a great pleasure to have you here," she said, above the whirring of the machine, the barking of the terrier, the meowing of the kittens, the shrieks of the receptionist and the giggling of the Arab girls. "I hope we shall see you again."

"Au revoir, Mesdames," said the electrician, looking up at last from his fuse-box—and there's style for you.

The Soil or the Soul?

IN 2003, I think it was, they erected in the historic heart of Dublin a monument they nicknamed the Dublin Spike—a slim pinnacle of stainless steel, some 120 metres high, unadorned except for indeterminate markings near its base. It is a sort of metallic exclamation of the new Ireland, the startling Euro-Ireland that came into being during the first decade of the twenty-first century.

When I arrived in Dublin from Wales one day I chose a passer-by of particularly Irish appearance to ask what he thought of the Spike, and what its enigmatic markings meant. I chose well, for he replied grandiloquently, "It's a grand conception, finely executed, an interesting idea, so it is. Is it those squiggles at the bottom you're asking about? Why they're to demonstrate that the object has been pulled out, dragged out, so it has, from the very soil of Ireland."

"The soil, did you say, or the soul?" I queried.

"Ah, sure you've hit it on the head there, right on target, full marks—the soil or the soul, that's the be all and end of it"—and laughing very Irishly, his coat flapping, off he strode towards O'Connell Bridge.

"SO YOU'RE AWAY to Galway in the morning?" said my hostess that night. "Make it an early start, and the traffic situation will be convenient for you."

Was she joking? In my experience there is no moment of the night or day when the traffic situation of contemporary Dublin is convenient. The traffic situation of Dublin is permanently awful. If it is not the morning rush hour it is the day of the horse show. If the street is not closed because of a collision the bridge is under repair. Road works are never-ending, cranes, scaffolds and bulldozers are all over the place, and only the slinky new street-cars glide through the clogged hubbub with a maddening air of privilege. Yet the unexpected thing, to anyone more accustomed to the movements of an older Ireland, is that it all happens without fuss or fluster. The Dubliners take it in their stride. It seems to me that modernity suits the Irish temperament, and against all historic expectations, thrives here like potatoes.

That glittering Spike tells us so! Like the monument itself, the new prosperity of the Republic, shiny, brash and confident, seems to have erupted out of the very substance of the country: and having erupted, feels natural to the place. One year Ireland was a poor and picturesque backwater, weighed down by its history and apparently sustained only by high jinks and alcohol. The next year, as it seems, it had become a brilliantly successful young State, a natural leader for all the small and minority nations of the world, and the first in Europe—would you believe it?—to ban smoking from all public working spaces.

It is a seriously rich country now, not only the second most expensive within the euro currency zone (after Finland) but the one most likely, economists say, to catch up with the United States in average personal wealth. The cars that fill Dublin fill all the cities of Ireland, and swarm into every last cranny of the countryside, so that wherever you drive, up the remotest mountain lane, down the narrowest track, there is likely to be another car in the rear mirror.

Thousands upon thousands of new houses have transformed the look of Ireland. Around every town they lie in regimented swathes, housing the multitudes who have escaped the old rural way of life, and speckled all over the landscape are bungalows and villas of grander aspiration, with conservatories and porte-cochères and ornamental eagles on gateposts. One and all seem brand-new. Even ancient cottages are spanking with fresh whitewash, plastic window frames, and burglar alarms, and no new house in the world is half so white, neat and spotless as a new house in Ireland. This old country of peasant values is being transformed, even as we watch, into a country of the aspiring bourgeoisie. Gone the squire and the yokel alike! Bring in the middle management!

It is a social as well as an economic revolution, but it does not strike me as a triumph of the *nouveaux riches*. It is more like an emancipation—more like Australia in the years when immigrants from continental Europe abruptly altered the mores of the country after the Second World War. The commuter suburbs of the new Ireland, with their trendy bistros, delicatessens, boutiques and garden centres, remind me of the burgeoning Sydney or Melbourne of those years, just as the proud new householders of Kildare and Kerry, with their sprinklers in the garden and Mercedes at the door, are like the Mediterranean entrepreneurs who so shook up the Aussies half a century ago.

Tourism of course is mighty in Ireland (where isn't it?), but it hasn't overwhelmed the place. Places like the Ring of Kerry which were beset by jaunting-cars in Victorian times are congested with tour coaches now; ageing folk musicians haunt the locations once beloved of auntly water-colourists; but few places in Ireland have become unbearably touristy, and in many the garish corrosion of the trade does not show at all. A myriad developers cherish frightful plans for the exploitation of Ireland, but so far their most horrific schemes for visitor centres or theme parks have been thwarted.

I suspect, all the same, that the Irish care more than they used to about what the world thinks of them. Keeping Ireland Tidy has become such a national preoccupation that when I drove into Aughrim, The Tidiest Town in Wicklow, I nearly turned and fled, so terrifyingly tidy was it. Some of the old reckless panache has undoubtedly been damped down, and it could hardly be otherwise, when Tidiness is all around you, and you have to skulk shamefaced in the street outside the pub if you want to have a smoke with your pint.

I am not complaining. Plenty of Irish people are, of course— mourning lost traditions, apprehensive of future prospects, worried about drugs and crime, wary of dubious motives. "If you only knew," they darkly say, when you ask about the manipulation of planning permissions, or the rising cost of living. During my visit the Irish Brewers' Association claimed that pubs had sold seven million fewer pints in the previous month because of the smoking ban. The sudden new pace of life, together with a drastic decline in religious faith, has inevitably brought its own stresses to a populace once so easygoing; I was sad to see that the intercession books in Irish churches reveal so often family tensions or new fears—"Sacred Mercies pray for my son Kevin to be well and drive carefully on the road," or "Holy Mother of God pray that Bridget and Kylie will be friends again."

Nevertheless, to an outsider from over the water what has happened to Ireland seems a twenty-first-century benediction. It is a spectacular display of materialism, indeed, but it is also a rare kind of epiphany: the moment when an entire nation, for so long a victim of cruel circumstance, is seizing history for itself at last, and starting all over again.

THE DUBLIN SPIKE breaks every rule of Irish convention. It is far too tall for its setting, and makes no attempt to blend with its handsome Georgian environment. An Taisce, the National Trust of Ireland, calls it "sterile," and so it is, in the sense that there is nothing fructifying to it. Yet to my mind it is absolutely right for its place and its moment, and its slender presence, erect above the urban scramble, seems properly to symbolize that constancy of the Irish spirit which amounts to—well, amounts to a soul.

There is a pub in the village of Borris, in County Carlow, which is a more immediate exhibition of constancy. It has been run by members of the O'Shea family since 1934, and began as one of those small emporia, saloon, grocer and hardware store all in one, that used to be characteristic of the Irish country town. The O'Shea business has never been disconcerted by progress. It has developed into a mini-supermarket, but is true as ever to its origins: behind the bar counter are stacked ancient packets of nails, or wire, or candles, which look as though they have been there since the store began, but which are still for sale, so the present Mr. O'Shea assures me, "if any customer asks." Children merrily sit on bar stools, ancients demolish Guinness and beef sandwiches, and if you happened to look in uninformed you might think nothing much had changed in Ireland since the 1950s.

Not that nostalgia is rampant in this republic. Not a soul has spoken to me about any good old days. In the country towns especially, nevertheless, one feels the mellowed presence of the past. The suburbs burgeon all around, but in the town square the shops are still one and all family concerns, ornately announced, and in the hotel middle-aged ladies in flowered frocks still gossip hilariously over their coffees, below portraits of the heroes who lodged there long ago—Robert Emmet or Collins "The Big Feller," Parnell Our Lost Leader, Daniel O'Connell the Liberator. The Catholic church of Our Lady of Mercy stands prosperously with its doors open, unfazed by scandals: the Protestant Church of St. John has been turned into a tourist office.

For the remains have almost vanished of the Protestant Ascendancy, the old hegemony which did so much, for better or for worse, to create the modern legend of Irishness. If you want a last taste of it, try the village of Castletownshend, down on the Cork coast. There, from the seventeenth to the twentieth century, three or four Anglo-Irish families were dominant, and their church is magnificently redolent of their presence—enormous plaques commemorate admirals, Etonians, Light Dragoons, Generals of the Bombay Army or aides-de-camp to Queen Victoria, and among them all is Edith Somerville of the famous literary partnership Somerville and Ross, who is described as Author, Artist, Musician and Master of Foxhounds, and who "played the organ in this church for 70 years." It is only a shadow now, that once splendiferous society, but here and there one sees the burned-out hulk of a great mansion, deserted since the independence wars, and on the hill above Castletownshend still live the descendants of Admiral Boyle Somerville, Royal Navy, murdered by the IRA in his own house in 1936.

But the twenty-first-century Irish appear to bear no grudges, and hardly seem to differentiate between the people of multitudinous nationalities who live and work all across the island. "Are you Lithuanian?" I asked a garage attendant at Ennis, in a wild guess. "No," she replied without a trace of surprise, "I am Ukrainian, but my husband is Lithuanian." Bewley's coffee shop in Dublin, a holy of traditional holies, is given even more style nowadays by its dizzily cosmopolitan range of employees, and foreign students are enrolled in every kind of school, from majestic Trinity College, Dublin, to the shadiest backstreet academy of computer technology. Across the island towns and hamlets proudly announce improbable foreign connections—Tallow, for instance, is Host Town to Bolivia, Rathdrum to Bahrain.

If there is one quality that has certainly survived the Irish transformation, it is the geniality of the people. They may be horribly ambitious in private, dubious of tactic and greedy, but in public they remain all Irish charm. "No problem," is their happy watchword, and there is nowhere else in the world, I swear, where a foreigner can so soon be made to feel at home. Irish road signage is not the most lucid, but it is a pleasure to ask the way, anyway, for the sake of the conversation.

O, wander this island for a week or two, through its legendary haze of mist and sunshine, fact and fiction, and wherever you go you will find the old Ireland living on! They are still singing, talking, drinking and playing the fiddle in the pubs of Galway— and if the weather is fine, still smoking on the sidewalks outside. . . . They are still making grand fruit-cake and marmalade to sell at the village hall of Roundwood, high in the Wicklow hills, and over the road in the church a sign still cries, "It's me again, O Lord!" In enclaves of Cork as in Connemara the Gaelic language struggles gamely on.

The Irish may be less rash and racy than they used to be, but the children's playground by the Powerscourt waterfall offers such a marvellous variety of potential injuries as to make many a health and safety specialist give up in despair. I had a room in Ennis the other night which overlooked a school yard, and watching the boisterous shenanigans down there, which looked like innocent frolic but were probably laced with childish malice, was like watching a stage performance of traditional Irish comedy.

Thrift in Ireland used to mean a bag of coins under the bed, or a miser in a short story. It is now expressed in equities and mortgage rates, and the foreign money that pours into Ireland comes because it will be safe and multiply. But it seems to me miraculous that a people so eagerly assuming the prosaic responsibilities of our age should retain so much of the merriment of the age before last. How many other States, great or small, can be described as fun?

I WENT BACK to the Dublin Spike before I left, and asked a passer-by of promisingly Irish appearance what she thought of the monument, and whether she considered it better represented the soil or the soul of Ireland. I had chosen her well, too, for she replied fluently, "It's a meaningless device, that's what it is, an awful waste of public money, a disgrace, so it is. And if I may say so, my dear, as to your second question, about the soil and the soul, that's a foolish thing to ask—what would the one be without the other?" And away she briskly stepped, fiercely swinging her shopping bag, in the direction of the General Post Office.

You've made that woman up, I hear you saying, that woman is pure invention. Ah yes, and so she is, so she is—but only just.

A Man in a Wine Bar

LONG AGO IN a Fleet Street wine bar, in London, a man named
Caradog Prichard was pointed out to me as a curiosity. He was
a well-respected Welsh journalist on the *Daily Telegraph*, I was
told, but also an eminent poet in the Welsh language. He had
left his traditional village in the mountains of north Wales when
he was no more than a boy, they said, he had lived in London for
many years, and his widowed mother had long been immured in
a lunatic aslyum. They certainly sounded curious circumstances,
but Prichard looked ordinary enough to me, middle-aged, amiable and evidently gregarious, and so far as I can remember I
never thought of him again until years later I read his esoteric
masterpiece *Un Nos Ola Leuad*—translated into English as *One
Moonlit Night*.

No book was ever truer to its author, no title ever more exact.

THAT "TRADITIONAL VILLAGE in the mountains" they had mentioned in the wine bar was in fact the substantial slate quarrying town of Bethesda, where Prichard was born in 1904. His quarryman father was killed at work there when Caradog was five months old, leaving his mother to raise him and two elder brothers in conditions of harsh poverty. Prichard left the place when he was an adolescent, first to work as a journalist on local papers, later to go to London, and since the early 1920s his mother had been a patient in a mental hospital at Denbigh, dying there in 1954.

Throw in two years of Army and Government service during and after the Second World War, and there you surely have a lifetime of embittering sadness, enough to make a neurotic misanthrope of a saint. Despite his sociable character, despite a happy marriage and success both as a journalist and as a poet, Prichard was tragically scarred within. He was plagued by suspicion that his father, who had been a strike-breaker in a prolonged and virulent quarry strike of the 1900s, had not been killed by accident, but had been murdered by resentful fellow workers. He became obsessed by the notion of suicide, and once tried to kill himself. He had bouts of heavy drinking. He was tormented by the thought of his poor mad mother struggling to keep her family clothed and fed. He was undoubtedly afflicted, like so many Welsh people who have chosen to live in exile, by pangs of homesickness and perhaps of guilt.

Yet the miracle is this: that *Un Nos Ola Leuad* is essentially a sweet-natured book, seldom bitter, often funny, and in the end ambiguously serene. It was first published in 1961, long after the events it evokes, and long after I had seen Prichard in the wine bar. At that time established literary sensibilities in Wales were being cruelly knocked askew by the general debunking of old assumptions—the emergence of a Welsh avant-garde, in fact; but although *Un Nos Ola Leuad* recorded suicide, sexual perversions, insanity, adulteries and murder in that village in the mountains, the book was an instant success among Welsh readers of all sorts. It was essentially a kind book, and perhaps that is why.

IT IS A sort of dream. Prichard himself described it as an "unreal picture, seen in the twilight and in the light of the moon," and it is illuminated throughout by a vision which, like moonlight itself, seems disorienting, casting too many shadows, throwing too many structures into sudden relief. De Chirico might have illustrated it, with figures by the elder Brueghel.

On the face of things the one logical thread of the work is provided by its narrative structure. It tells the story of one day and one night, and it is told by a single, unnamed voice. But it turns out to be far from simple, because although the voice is that of a boy, sometimes it apparently speaks with the experience of a grown man, and three times in the course of the book it is superseded by eerily vatic pronouncements of no explicable origin.

These are couched in lofty poetical language, rather like divine interjections in Homer, and are all the more unsettling because at all other times the narrative voice is touchingly naïve. It expresses itself throughout not merely in a broad north Walian

vernacular, the lingua franca of the Bethesda quarry communities, but also in the vocabulary and intonation of a child. He is
a particularly engaging child, too, innocently ready for fun and
harmless mischief but precociously tender in his sympathies. He
is grateful for small kindnesses. He is devoted—perhaps over-
devoted—to his widowed mother. There is something wistful
about him, one feels, which sets him apart from his fellows, and
gives to those Olympian interruptions a fateful suggestion of
premonition.

And it presently becomes clear that the premonition is of mad-
ness. The very first paragraph of the book suggests it, with an
incongruous touch of the liturgical and something very strange
about its tone of voice:

> I'll go and ask Huw's Mam if he can come out to play. Can
> Huw come out to play, O Queen of the Black Lake? No, he
> can't, he's in bed and that's where you should be you little
> monkey, instead of going round causing a riot at this time
> of night. Where were you two yesterday making mischief
> and driving village folk out of their minds?

WHERE THE TWO were yesterday is to be the ostensible theme
of the book, but the village folk out of their minds and the Black
Lake are to be with us to the end. In the first twenty-five pages
of *Un Nos* we come across a sadistic schoolmaster, an epileptic
having a fit, a woman threatening her husband with a bread knife,
a corpse brought home from a madhouse, a woman committed to
a madhouse, an eviction, rumours of sexual deviation, a woman

locked in a coal shed, violent fisticuffs outside the Blue Bell, a
couple fornicating in a wood, a horse dropping dead in its stable
and somebody hanging himself in the lavatory. All this we witness through the sensibility of a small boy, more puzzled than
aghast at what he sees, and when on page 25 he goes to bed on a
bright moonlit night, tucked up with his Mam for comfort, God
knows what we can expect in the morning.

> There's a full moon tonight. Why won't you let Huw come
> out to play, O Queen of the Black Lake?

AS THE BOY wanders the town that day, he remembers events
of his life: but as he wanders he grows older, too, and although
he still speaks as a child he seems to see as an adult. Sometimes
he is one age, sometimes he is another, and it is both as boy and
as man that he recalls the tragedies of his childhood—the deaths
of his two best friends, the loss of his mother when she is taken
away to mental hospital, the cruel grotesqueries of village life,
the poverty and the presence somewhere of that ominous lake.
As we peer through the moonlight, we gradually realize that we
are witnessing a slow descent into insanity.

How much is real in the narrative, how much is hallucination,
we never discover. When we set foot at last upon the banks of
the Black Lake, we know we are in the company of a murderer,
but how old he is, whether he is free or incarcerated, whether he
is sane or crazy, just about to enter an abyss or recently escaped
from one—all these questions are left so mistily unresolved that
we wonder whether the author himself, in his unnamed persona

as the Bethesda child, or as that unremarkable customer in the Fleet Street wine bar, ever knew the answers.

And yet . . . I come back to *Un Nos Ola Leuad* time and again not for the tragedy of it, or even the haunting mystery, but for the sweet pity of it all.

The Nijinski of Grammar

TO MY MIND every letter of the alphabet, every punctuation mark, has its own resonances. The letter *b*, for example, is especially suited to abuse—the words "bastard," "blithering," "brute," "bitch," "bully," are just made to be blurted out with blustering bravado. And surely nothing could be more absolutely final than a full stop—a period to Americans—with no compromising tail or ingratiating squiggle to weaken its decision. Be off with you, you beastly boy, booms the letter *b*. Right, that's it, clearly declares the full stop, end of story.

The most sensitive of these grammatical symbols, and the most crudely threatened by ignorant fashion, is the exclamation mark, as graceful in allegory as it is in appearance. Lily-like is how the exclamation mark appears to me, sensual, fastidious, but every year fewer practitioners dare to employ it. It is true that its purposes have long been cheapened, so that it is nicknamed "the scream," is splashed across the pages of schoolgirl love letters, and is a stock-in-trade of satirists. Throughout the English-speaking world editors routinely remove exclamation marks, as though they are signs of illiteracy, or at least insults to the house style.

But in my opinion this elegant device is one of the glories of literary usage. In some languages letters mutate to conform with the word that follows them. The exclamation mark remains the same whatever the thought it is illustrating, but its meaning miraculously shifts. It is like a written tone of voice. It can be, of course, exclamatory, but it can also magically signify humour, horror, sarcasm and a host of other emotions. It is, one might say, the Nijinski of grammar!

And there, in that very use of it, its virtuosity is illustrated. I am employing it in that sentence because I intend the remark to be surprising, amusing and perhaps a little ironic. But in just the same context it could also express shock, or dismay, or contempt, or ridicule, or just exclamation—"Dear God! The Nijinski of grammar!" I even find it useful as a sort of emollient; thrown into a letter of reproach, it can soften the temper of everything, adding an ameliorating flicker of amusement or complicity. In short, you can do almost anything with the exclamation mark. You can triple or quadruple it if you want to express hilarity, or, especially if you are in grade ten, emphasize your undying devotion to somebody. Spaniards turn it upside-down, and print it one way at the start of a sentence, the other way at the end. In some countries it stands, all by itself, as an extremely effective all-purpose traffic warning, and artists of comic strips long ago recognized its explosive effect, especially in combination with multiple asterisks.

For me, though, it is above all a thing of beauty. There it stands now, top left on my computer keyboard, and it makes all else look vulgar, especially that bloody *b*.

Scots in a Train

WHERE ARE WE? The train is spotless, bright and fast. The youth who comes round with the food trolley sounds exquisitely educated. The ticket collecter is urbanely courteous. All the other passengers are equally charming, and smile happily if you smile at them. Where in the unlovely world are we? We are in the blue-and-white electric train that runs every fifteen minutes between Glasgow and Edinburgh, the principal cities of one of Europe's most civilized small countries, Scotland.

SUCH TRAVEL BONHOMIE is rare these days, and it arises perhaps from the famously celebratory character of both cities. At the great Edinburgh Art Festival, for instance, hordes of artists, writers, actors, comedians, pundits and musicians perform, squabble, philosophize and pose until the dawn breaks. At Glasgow thousands of enthusiasts, boisterous and sentimental, gather for the international piping festival, and then too the last drone of the bagpipes will not fade away until long after the pubs have closed. The nature of these jamborees, the one so cerebral, the other so visceral, says a lot about the nature of Scotland, and so do the cities themselves.

Edinburgh is the Scottish capital, and looks like it. Grey, elegant, castle-crowned, it is just made for kings and glory. It is the seat of the national Parliament, its daily newspaper is called simply *The Scotsman*, Scottish flags fly all over it and when I bought a little volume there called *100 Best Scottish Books* I was only mildly surprised to find that the titles listed included Conrad's *Heart of Darkness* and the Holy Bible.

In Glasgow I would be more likely to find *1000 Best Glasgow Jokes* or *Your Wee Dictionary of Glaswegian*. Glasgow is like a City-State, staunchly parochial in its prides, feisty in historical attitudes. For years the most popular exhibit in its Museum of Modern Art was a figure of Queen Elizabeth II, crowned and ermined, smoking a fag and holding the morning's milk bottles under one arm, the day's tabloid under the other.

But both are very ancient cities, both unmistakably Scottish, and they complement each other in an ornery kind of way, so that it is easy enough to imagine the young avant-gardists getting pissed in Glasgow, the hearty pipers soaking up post-deconstructionist reggae in Edinburgh.

"ARE WE NEARLY THERE?" The universal cri de coeur is
politely expressed on the Scotrail express, and easily answered.
Bless you, chick, we are already there. Scotland itself exists in the
balance between its two splendid cities, and all around us as we
speed towards one or the other, everything Scottish accompanies
us: the mountains and the lochs, the great ships and the kilted
soldiers, heather and whisky and Adam Smith and the red-nosed
comics of tradition—all are with us already, my love, all around
us, as the train speeds on and that obvious young Master of
Arts (a very good second-class degree, without a doubt) offers
us another slice of cake from his trolley.

Paradise Somewhere

IF PARADISE IS the stuff of the conventional promise, all sweet-meats and complaisant houris, then I certainly have never experienced it. But a nirvana of a different kind I did transiently enter long ago, when I was on my way back to Kathmandu, in Nepal, out of the Himalayas. I was travelling with a Sherpa friend of mine. His name was Sonam. We had come out of the mountains fast, and when we got down into the foothills I began to feel ill and weak—the reverse of altitude sickness, I suppose. The monsoon had broken upon us, and the endless rain did not help, but "Come with me to my home village," Sonam said, "and we will make you better."

The village was only a few miles off our route, and it was called Chaunrikharka. At the time I only knew of it by the sound of it, because I had never seen the name on a map, or read any reference to it. In those days I doubt if any European had ever set foot in the place, and to this day it remains in my mind hardly more than a mellifluous suggestion, with a name that sounds lovely but is the very devil to spell.

Like most Sherpa villages then, it was just a cluster of small huts surrounded by potato fields and gardens, with nothing in the way of a focus, no school or public temple—nothing to make a hard fact of it, as it were, as against a blurred recollection. We got there at dusk, and to me it all seemed just a misty sort of *somewhere*. A great snow peak rose somewhere above the village. A tumbling river rushed somewhere below. Sonam's family house was somewhere in the middle of the place, and he led me to an upstairs room somewhere in the shambled wooden structure, unrolled my sleeping-bag for me somewhere on the floor and introduced me to my one experience of paradise—somewhere, somewhere or other, in the Himalaya foothills of Nepal.

The long room was very dark, and at one end of it was the Sonam family shrine. A dozen small images of the Buddha stood there in an alcove, attended by flickering butter candles, and as I remember there was no other furniture. Everything was woody, smoky, creaky, flickering and inexact. Outside the rain fell steadily, with a heavy swishy noise, and I soon fell into what I suppose now was a feverishly debilitated sleep. When I woke up next day the first thing I saw was that shrine, gently luminous in the morning light, and I found myself almost hallucinatorily happy. It was still raining, but life was in full fling all around me. Outside my door the fields stood green, fresh and gleaming in the wet, and a marvellously suggestive vegetable smell reached me—part fertile, part rotten, part bitter, part sweet, past its best but already renewing itself, like a subliminal and oddly comforting text of existence. The river still rushed, but mingled with its noise was the hilarious laughter of children, the shrill merry gossip of Sherpa women, the clatter of pans and the cheerful voice of Sonam, clumping up the outside steps to see how I was.

Was it two nights I spent there? Was it two years? It might have been either, because time lost meaning for me in Chaunrikharka. All the many Sonams visited me in my convalescence, some young and rosy, some extremely old, sometimes singly, sometimes all at once, feeding me roast potatoes and dosing me with the powerful white liquor called *rakhsi*, which plays a happy part in the Sherpa culture. Strangers sporadically appeared at my open door to peer kindly and wonderingly at me. The rain hissed and clattered, on the fields and on the roof, and the women talked and talked downstairs.

And always, throughout my stay, those serene images of the alcove looked gently back at me, and the candles flickered, guttering when a gust of wind blew through or under my door. I heard not a harsh word. I saw not an unfriendly face. I grew to love the spatter of rain on the roof, and the scents of woodsmoke and vegetables, and the bright inquisitive eyes of the innumerable grubby brown infants invited in by junior Sonams to take a look at me.

When I was better they showed me around the fields, and took me to the roaring river, and introduced me to the neighbours, who completed my cure with lavish tin mugs of *rakhsi*. When the time came to resume our journey, a covey of urchins came with us for the first few hundred yards, prancing and tumbling and laughing all around us, and I thought they provided a properly dream-like *envoi* to a transcendental interlude.

For more than fifty years I half-wondered if my stay in the

somewhere of Chaunrikharka was a purely imaginary enchant-
ment, born by fever out of exhaustion. It was only the other
day that, examining a new map of eastern Nepal, I discovered
for certain that my momentary paradise had existed, east of the
Dudh Kosi river, west of the snow peak Gonglha, due south of
Phakdingma.

Three

Smug revenge upon the merry

On to Maturity!

OH, THE JOYLESSNESS of the word "maturity"! Nobody ever cried "On, on to Maturity!," with a reckless flourish of flags or opinions. Nobody ever wrote that to be mature was perfect heaven. During my time in journalism, when the trade was politer than it is now, the word "mature" went with "ample" (meaning fat), "attractive" (meaning plain) or "vivacious" (meaning garrulous), in the news-room vocabulary of euphemisms. In the wider social world, it spoke of settling down, early nights, the pram in the hall, prudence, mortgages, reality and common sense. President Truman of the United States, tiring of the mature reflections of his financial advisers—"On the one hand, Mr. President, but then again, on the other . . ."—said that what he wanted was a one-armed economist, and I know just what he meant.

With maturity we enter the lecture hall of academe, its truest dwelling place and to my mind the most dread of chambers. Here the meridian torture awaits us, even those who, like me, are experienced at reading frivolous novels while the presiding sage drones on (for however hardened we are, however thick-skinned, still we cannot help feeling the bloodless disapproval of the other people in the row). Maturity in the lecture kind is the devil's smug revenge upon the merry.

Of course the adjective "mature" need not be pejorative. Applied to wine it speaks of mellowness, sublety, ease and grace. But even then it is not for me. The wines I like best are young, sharp and mischievous, the sort that ought really to be warmed a bit, except that I cannot wait—wines beneath the notice of the connoisseurs who, in the infinite complacency of their analyses, are the very essence of the mature. "You may not appreciate it now," I hear one such savant telling some brash young adolescent, "but you will appreciate its grandeur when you are older." When he is more mature, the old fraud means, when the sap is subsiding, when the first fine rapture has been dulled by maturity . . .

What about a mature cheese? It tends to stink. Or a mature judgement? It takes an age to ripen. Mature students go to lectures. When a bill matures, you have to pay it. There was a famous actor called Mature, when I was immature myself, and I am surprised that he never chose a *nom de théâtre* for himself. Perhaps only family loyalty dissuaded him from an immortality with more panache—the name was doubtless fine for his dad George Marcellus Mature, cutler, of Louisville, Kentucky, but surely not for Victor Mature, film star, of Hollywood, California . . . !

In short, I do not like the adjective "mature," because I resent the noun it has bred. Maturity! Maturity! Did ever a heart thrill to the sound of it, still less the meaning? There was a time when I actually congratulated myself on becoming mature, earning the respect of my experience, and throwing off the callowness of youth. No longer! Give me callowness every time, give me fizz, give me irresponsibility, and if ever I feel maturity creeping in, crack a bottle, put out more flags and ring the bells!

Steamboat Pleasures

IF EVER YOU pine for the old bourgeois pleasures, genteel, discreet, complacent and in my own case fondly imperialist pleasures, get you to Lake Lucerne in Switzerland, and board one of the five glorious paddle-steamers which have been sailing those waters since the early years of the last century.

Make straight for the dining saloon, and there over a cup of coffee you will be eased into nirvana. Port and starboard the mountains rise above the lake, dappled even in summer, with recalcitrant patches of snow. The woodwork creaks around you, the pistons pound below, the paddles gently swish, there is a faint smell of engine oil and presently a breathy blast of the ship's horn tells you that you are approaching the little lakeside resort of Weggis.

Relax. No hurry to finish your coffee. Weggis is a very haven of those patient bourgeois pleasures, and the captain of the

Schiller (319 tons, built in 1906) will be tolerantly smiling down at you from his bridge when you are the last to disembark, before with another toot of the siren his ship swims like a punctual swan away.

WE CALL IT Lake Lucerne, but it is really Vierwaldstätter See, the Lake of the Four Forest Cantons, and it lies in the very heart of the virtual Switzerland we are seeking: not the real Switzerland, an immensely competent and hard-headed little State, equipped with every modernity. but the Switzerland of our more languid fancies, where ships' captains wave goodbye from the wheelhouses of centenarian steamboats, amiable porters greet you at the doors of unostentatiously comfortable hotels, and distant music sounds from municipal bandstands on Tuesday mornings.

It is quite likely to be gypsy music of some kind, but played in a decidedly un-Romany manner—no foot-stampings here, no cries of ecstasy or final triumphant waving of fiddle-bows. The audience is attentive, appreciative, even affectionate in its responses, but certainly not reckless. Average ages are high in Weggis, and the prevailing temper is kind but undemonstrative.

It is true that small boys sometimes somersault into the lake from the steamer landing, when the *Schiller*, the *Uri* (built 1901), the *Unterwalden* (1902), the *Gallia* (1913) or the *Stadt Luzern* (1928) is nowhere about. True, too, that sometimes shoppers and secretaries trundle insouciantly past on roller-skates, and stalwart soldiers of the Swiss Army clump through town in their camouflage gear and big boots. But the general mood of the place is placid, or perhaps valetudinarian.

Certainy Weggis is very concerned with health. "Wellness" is its leitmotif—in English, and with capital *W*s. There are Wellness hotels and Wellness restaurants, Wellness diets, Wellness habits, and everywhere there are Wellness people walking, in varying degrees of exertion, with those Nordic walking poles. Believe me, by the time you have been in Weggis for a day or two you are likely to be either lying on a *chaise-longue* at the lake's edge, wiggling your toes (if it is a Tuesday) to the beat of *The Merry Widow* from the bandstand, or are ambling the foreshore on your Nordic walking poles.

Or eating. Sad to say, probably not fish out of the lake—even the Vierwaldstätter See can be polluted—but robust healthy meals with lots of vegetables, and good Swiss wine to go with them. The local people seldom seem to be fat, and this I attribute partly to the diet, partly to the lovely mountain air, and partly perhaps to Nordic walking poles.

AND PARTLY TO the atttitude of meticulous regularity that comes with those ancient steamboats. The church bells of Weggis ring comfortingly throughout the night from the fourteenth-century tower of the parish church, but during the day it is the arrival of the steamers that gives the town its reassuring sense of order. Not all the ships of the Schifffahrtsgesellschaft des Vierwaldstättersees are venerable paddle-steamers: some are sleek modern motor vessels with Klaxon horns and revvable engines. They are the sounds and suggestions of the steamboats, though, that dictate the life rhythm of Weggis, its citizens, and not least its visitors.

There you are, recumbent in the garden of the Beau Rivage Hotel, say, which has been attending to our needs under one name or another since the early seventeenth century. All is calm, all is Swiss, ducks doze upon the jetty, and at one o'clock somebody is going to bring you an omelette to eat in the multicoloured gazebo at the water's edge. You are half-asleep, perhaps, awaiting the gentle summons to your victuals, but just before the moment arrives you hear the chunk-chunk of paddles, and a thoughtful touch of a steam-whistle, and almost simultaneously three things occur: the church clock strikes one, the *Stadt Luzern* docks, and a sweet soft voice says your omelette awaits you.

In between the hours, too, the impeccable coming and going of the steamers is like some pledge of eternity. At summer weekends the Vierwaldstätter See is a restless pageant of water life. Hundreds of yachts are tacking all across the lake. Speedboats scud about. Excursion boats are jammed with tourists. Anglers are out there with their rods and nets, and everywhere small white pleasure craft with parasols are sidling along the wooded shorelines below the mountains. But among them, every now and then, there stalks one of those grand old ships, stately and silent in the distance, with a rim of white around its prow, the faintest shimmer of heat haze from its rakish smokestack, and a constant, purposeful flurry of foam beneath its paddle-boxes, as though Time itself could not deter its passage.

FOR THE GREATHEART paddle-steamers of Lake Lucerne are not only splendours in their own right; they are integral to the ethos of the Vierwaldstätter See, to the ethos of precise respectability that we have come here to enjoy. Long after you have left the lake, when the corrosion of the great world is all around you once more, you will still hear their sirens sounding, see their captains lordly on their bridges, and remember the delicately fattening sweetness of the cakes in their saloons.

Mark Twain, that old river pilot, undoubtedly responded to their magic, even then—he thought a steamboat voyage on Lake Lucerne "almost the perfection of pleasuring." And perhaps Kipling the romantic had an echo of them in his mind, as I do now, when he wrote about those imperial paddle-wheels chunking from Rangoon to Mandalay.

Invisible Loyalty

IT WAS ALLEGORY with a vengeance when, in the first decade of the twenty-first century, the cartographers of the European Union decided that Wales did not exist, and struck it (inadvertently perhaps) from the map. For Welsh patriots of my persuasion, though, no worries. We know that since the beginnings of history ours has been, as often as not, a country of the mind, a homeland of the imagination, a love-land if you like, impervious to the vulgarities of map-makers and politicians.

Besides, our traditions are full of places that have sunk without trace, or are temporarily invisible. Castled islands irrevocably subside into lakes, remembered in a bubbly way only by subaqeous chimes of bells at midnight. Swathes of land are swallowed by the sea—if you are suitably constituted, like me, you may still distinctly detect them shining on the western horizon. Lord bless you, in proper Welsh weather it often feels as though the country is about to be submerged anyway, and it doesn't discourage us—good for the character, we say.

For of course the prospect of elimination has been with the Welsh nation for generations—if not extinction by drowning, then expungement by history. Removal from the rest of the United Kingdom, which the EU visionaries apparently foresee, is for many of us no threat at all. I myself often love to dream that we have somehow been geologically detached, and have drifted south-westward into the Irish Sea, to a location somewhere between Cornwall and Cork.

FOR MANY ENGLISH people too the disappearance of Wales from the map would be no disaster, although to be fair to them they are generally thinking of political rather than physical maps. As the London *Daily Telegraph* observed in 1860, it was only "a small country, unfavourably situated, with an indifferent soil and inhabited by an unenterprising people." The Prime Minister Herbert Asquith once said that he would rather go to hell than visit the western flank of the kingdom, and it is well known (though apocryphal, I fear) that the entry for Wales in the *Encyclopaedia Britannica* used to read simply: See England.

It was not always a joke, and isn't now. English policy was for centuries directed towards the absorption of Wales into England, and has repeatedly been nearly successful. The ancient Welsh culture, which is unique to itself, has been at one time or another almost overwhelmed by the sheer presence of its insatiable neighbour, the mightiest cuckoo in all the nests of history.

Heirs to the English throne were impertinently dubbed Princes of Wales, when as often as not they seldom came near the place if they could help it. English bishops and clergymen swarmed over Welsh parishes. English landowners occupied huge estates, living ineffably English lives.

Above all, the English tried to stifle that essential inspiration of Welshness, Cymraeg, the Welsh language. In churches, in schools, in courts of law, in every aspect of Government, the language was ignored, despised or where possible extinguished. Nothing is more bitterly remembered among Welsh patriots, to this day, than the humiliating "Welsh Not," the sign that was hung around the neck of any pupil heard speaking the Welsh language in nineteenth-century Welsh schools.

It is a miracle that it has never happened. The most determined of the Welsh remain just as Welsh still. The language remains indestructible. Few English people, I think, would now wish Wales to be struck from the map, and on the whole, as far as I can make out, few of them care much about Welsh independence from the United Kingdom. The worst attitude they display towards Welshness is one of frivolous contempt, expressed in adolescent humour by comedians and journalists: this is due, as we all know, to their national sense of inferiority, and is best dealt with by a proper *noblesse oblige*.

I LAUGH, BUT that map may well come metaphorically true. Welsh patriots know that even now the Welsh identity is maintained only by a ceaseless resistance to every inroad from across Offa's Dyke—assaults made immensely more powerful nowadays by England's subservience to everything American. Anglo-America, or rather Amer-England, is the threat to their survival now, and as all its manifestations pour insidiously and inexorably across our defenceless frontier, Wales may yet disappear by sheer force of osmosis.

There are people in the Welshest parts of Wales who are made so profoundly unhappy by the whittling away of their language, their values and their ways of life that they are driven to alcoholism, driven to nervous breakdown. It is not only incoming ideas and examples that are doing it to them: it is incoming people. They may be accused of racism, but as they see whole villages, whole districts virtually taken over by newcomers, with the best will in the world (and the Welsh are the kindest of people) they can only wish to God the English would stay at home in Wolverhampton or Basingstoke. "Welcome to Wales," says the slogan of one resistance movement. "Enjoy your Stay, Then Go Away."

In Wales tourism, the badge or front of almost any country nowadays, is already very largely in the hands of English people, from the country pub to the allegedly posh hotel (not very posh, actually). Nearly every corner shop is gone. Half the post offices are in English hands. And the vast tide of English families means that even the schools, where the Welsh language is part of the curriculum, become more Amer-anglicized every term—for every incoming child who becomes Welsh, half a dozen Welsh-speaking children no longer speak Welsh in the playground. Every day of the year another few hundred Welsh houses of the Welsh countryside are sold to English people for prices that very few Welsh country people can afford, more often than not to become bridgeheads of cultural corrosion.

FOR MYSELF, HALF Welsh, half English, I am certainly no racist, and I am only just a nationalist nowadays, because I no longer believe in nationality, or in the cursed Nation-State. I am however a culturalist, and I fear that peoples must achieve Statehood if they are to preserve their very selves. To my mind it would be a dreadful tragedy if small peoples like ours were in fact to disappear from the map—not the geographical map, which probably won't happen for a million years or so, but the political map, which might happen anytime.

But I dare say those cartographers of the Eurostat Political Compendium were subconsciously expressing a truth when they consigned Wales to oblivion. In a way ours is already an invisible country, or at least a hidden country. "As soon as we came into the pub," say English raconteurs when they get home again, "those people started jabbering in Welsh." Nonsense. They were jabbering in Welsh long before you came in, before your forebears even crossed the Severn, and believe me, they will be jabbering still when you are gone.

For much of the Welsh culture is private. Countless poems are written, innumerable tales are told, songs are sung, customs honoured, jokes enjoyed, loyalties upheld, beyond the observation of visitors. Beneath its surface ours is a strong society still, commanding the love, no less, of hundreds of thousands of its people, whether they speak Welsh or not—for if they do not speak it on the tongue, most of them speak it in the instinct.

So go ahead, you map-makers of Europe. Strike us off, let us drift off your margin. We know you mean no harm, and have probably just pressed the wrong button on your computer.

Anyway, if you come to Wales now you will find it half-submerged already: by the end of the century it may all be flooded. Listen, though, whenever you come, listen hard, dream a bit, and down there in the waters you will hear those bubbly bells still ringing.

Dreaming Dreams?

THIS IS WHAT I dreamed one night. It was a short dream. I dreamed that Elizabeth said to me, casually over our coffee, "By the way, when you held the paper up before your face before supper, was it because you were picking your nose, and didn't want me to see?"

I had to admit that it was. "I have to admit that it was. It's such an ugly thing to do, isn't it, but sometimes I find it necessary. My nose gets so stuffed up. Do you suppose everyone does it? Does the Queen pick her nose when nobody's looking?"

"I'm quite sure she does," Elizabeth said, and there the matter dropped.

But it was a dream that was not entirely a dream. Was it a dream at all? Elizabeth tells me that we had never had such a conversation, but I have to admit that I had in fact picked my nose before supper, and had indeed hidden myself shamefaced behind the paper. It is such an ugly thing to do, isn't it, though sometimes necessary even for the most fastidious. What has disturbed me about the little experience is its blending of sleep and wake, its accuracy so exact in some ways, so blurred in others, which has made me wonder where hallucination ended and memory began. Perhaps this overlap is true of most dreams: but I am beginning to wonder how much of it is true of life itself, and if the peculiarly easy, frank, inessential, glancing but conclusive nature of our exchange over the coffee is what dying is going to be like.

Why, I wonder, should this particular inconsequential dream lead me to such portentous speculation? Something out of childhood, you will doubtless say. It is true that I have one or two deeply ingrained phobias—for example, anything to do with candles, like candle-light dinners, or candle wax—which I can only explain to myself by supposing they were planted by some experience in infancy. And it is also true that one of my most vivid memories, not a dream at all, concerns picking one's nose.

WHENEVER I LIKE, if I close my eyes and think hard, I can feel myself to be back within the few square feet of space, part light, part shade, that lies beneath the archway of Tom Gate at Christ Church, Oxford. I have known it all my life, and whenever I please I can transport myself there. I'll do it now. Sure enough, here I am in that shadowy archway, beneath the majestic tower, and even now its bell Great Tom reverberates around me, striking the hour. On my left is a fluttering notice-board, and the usual jumble of bikes. On the right a stately porter in a bowler hat sits in his glass-windowed cubicle—the very same man, I swear it, who sat there in the 1930s, except that now he may be black. Students, dons and tourists sporadically pass through, and their progress in and out of the shadow of old Tom is like crossing a frontier.

For on one side the gate opens on to the tumultuous St. Aldate's Street, where the tide of the world thunders by, but on the other it admits its visitors to Tom Quad, one of the most magnificent quadrangles in Europe, regally serene and private. As I stand there half-way between the two it is like sniffing two drinks, a Heineken, say, and a burgundy, whose bouquets seep in from opposite directions but never quite blend. They used to call this dichotomy Town and Gown, but nowadays it is a confrontation more subtle.

"Can I help you?" says the porter in a meaningful way, seeing me loitering there, half in and half out of the shadows of the gate. Christ Church is a decidedly authoritarian establishment, founded in the first place by a cardinal and a king. But it is authority from the other side, the St. Aldate's side, the interference of the great world, of politicians and bureaucrats, of tabloids and ideologues, that I associate most pungently with Tom Gate. When I was eight or nine years old I was passing through the arch one day when I felt a tickle on my cheek, and scratched it with my finger as I walked.

At that moment there paraded down the pavement, walking in line ahead towards the police station along the street, half a dozen policemen, burly and helmeted in the manner of those days. They marched along, as they did then, in a semi-military way, and, with their antique helmets and their big boots, struck me as homely and rather comical. As they passed me, one of them spoke out of the corner of his mouth. "Don't pick your nose," he said.

I wasn't picking my nose! I was scratching my cheek! But I had no chance to remonstrate. The constables went clumping on, and seven decades later, as I meditate now, the resentment of that moment lives with me still. The unfairness of it! The arrogance! Perhaps it really is the emotion of that distant injustice, the latent dislike of authority that I feel to this day, which has obscurely linked the matter of nose-picking with the matter of mortality, via a short dream. Even if I had been picking my nose, what business was it of Mr. Plod? And why shouldn't I pick my nose now if I want to, whoever is watching, in my own house, at my age?

BUT I PROTEST too much. Shame enters my introspections. The habit of picking my nose only seized me, in fact, long years after that episode at Tom Gate, when a minor operation on my nose left it slightly disfunctional—unable to clear itself by the normal processes of blowing or, I imagine, natural dissolution. Ever since I have had to help it along by the unlovely process of picking it.

It's such an unlovely thing to do, isn't it, but d'you suppose everyone does it? I expect so, but since I am obliged to do so more often than most people, I am profoundly ashamed of it. As a matter of fact it is my only guilty secret, this unlovely habit. There have been times when I have been detected in the act. Passing motorists have caught sight of me picking my nose at the wheel, or at least I have thought they have, and although I have hastily scratched my cheek instead, and tried to persuade myself that they could not really have seen me, and will never see me again, and probably don't in the least care anyway, and are perhaps even gratified to find that somebody else does it too—even so, when they have flashed by, I am left ashamed of myself. It is such an ugly habit, isn't it?

I am not actually ashamed of shame, if you follow me. Shame can be a saving grace, and certainly a consolation. We feel better ourselves if we are ashamed of something we've done, and with luck a show of shame can reduce the sentence in the courtroom, where slower-witted justices can be persuaded that shame is synonymous with regret. "My client is truly ashamed, m'lud," counsel often successfully pleads, and he would have to be a moron to add "but, m'lud, he doesn't in the least regret it, and it would give him the greatest pleasure to do it again." Shame and regret are certainly not the same things: *je ne regrette rien*, like charity, can cover a multitude of sins.

Shame can operate as a prophylactic, too. I first heard the word "prophylactic" when, with my batch of innocent recruits to the wartime British Army, I was given a welcoming lecture about the pitfalls of sex. I confused the word in my mind with the little scrolls of sacred texts, phylacteries, that used to be carried in leather pouches around the foreheads of rabbis, until my cruder comrades made songs and jokes out of it, and it was years before I realized that it had nothing specifically sexual or Jewish about it, but merely meant a technique of preventive medicine.

The prophylaxis of shame can prevent bad behaviour before it happens. Often enough, like many another coward, I have been brave because I am ashamed to be frightened—or ashamed to look frightened perhaps, an even less admirable motive. Perhaps it's true of everyone. Buzz Aldrin, when he landed on the moon, may have been ashamed to look frightened on the Houston TV screens (but it would have been hard to judge, wouldn't it, through the little window of his helmet). I notice that shame, though it prevents me from picking my nose in public, does not invariably bring out my better self when I am all alone.

BUT HERE'S A thought. Perhaps I *was* picking my nose that day, when the policemen walked past Tom Gate! I remember with absolute clarity that I was only scratching my cheek, but what if I wasn't? It has been a dogma of my life that truth and imagination are not simply interchangeable but are often one and the same. Something imagined is as real, to my mind, as something one can touch or eat. A fanciful fear is as alarming as a genuine one, a love conceived as glorious as a love achieved. A virtual reality may only be in one's own mind, imperceptible to anyone else, but why is it any the less true for that? Music exists before its composer writes it down.

It is easy for writers, even writers of non-fiction, to think like this. Every sentence we create we have created from nothing, and made real, and every situation has been touched up in our memory. For years I remembered clearly how the roofs of Sydney Opera House hung like sails over the harbour when I first visited the city, until it was drawn to my attention that the Opera House hadn't been built then. Every place I ever wrote about became more and more my own interpretation of it, more and more an aspect of myself, until in the end I determined that

I was the city of Trieste, and Trieste was me, and decided it was time for me to give up.

I realized then that my dreams and my realities were merging. Could it be that much of what I had experienced in life I had not really experienced at all, except in my imagination? This was not at all an unpleasant conjecture—oddly soothing in fact, and it is what made me think that my dream about picking my nose, my shame about it, my secrecy, my denial, my realization that half was a dream and half wasn't, the easy resolution of the conundrum, the sensation that it didn't much matter anyway—all made me think that such a cloudy transition from one condition to another, or vice versa, might be what death will be like. If this essay is a muddle too, with its inconsequential repetitions—not at all my waking style—that is because I have allowed it to float along with the stream of instinct, among the weeds and little whirlpools, like Ophelia.

I always used to think that the most frightening words in literature were Hamlet's "perchance to dream"—

> *To die—to sleep.*
> *To sleep! perchance to dream! ay, there's the rub,*
> *For in that sleep of death what dreams may come . . . .*

For years I laughed at Ivor Novello, who used the phrase as the title of a frothy operetta. But now I think the dreams of death may turn out to be much like my dream of life, mysteries gradually dispersing, shames forgotten, truth and fancy reconciled, drifting downstream through the weeds and the reeds—lazily, as Lord Salisbury once said of British foreign policy, "and only occasionally putting out a boat-hook to avoid a collision."

O Manhattan!

"WHAT'S NEW?" I ingratiatingly asked the cab driver who picked me up at JFK. I had arrived to celebrate my fifty-odd years of acquaintance with Manhattan, and was making the conventional opening ploy. Answer, however, came there none. Either the driver spoke only Ruthenian, or he couldn't hear me above the rattle of his vehicle. I tried again. "How are things?" I said in my most fulsome Transatlantic, and this time he replied.

"Traffic is lousy in the tunnel, we take Queensboro and 59th, OK? You just sit back comfortable, right?"

This was music to my ears, and I relaxed as we bumped erratically out of the airport. Matthew Arnold once wrote of an infinitesimal pair of English villages that "in the two Hinkseys nothing keeps the same." I have always believed precisely the opposite of Manhattan, the ultimate world city.

So "Fine," said I, "thanks a million." For I felt that I had known that agreeable fellow all my life, that he had always come from some generic Ruthenia, that down the years he never had heard me the first time, that traffic in the Midtown Tunnel had been lousy every day at least since Idlewild became JFK, and that in Manhattan indeed nothing really does change.

THIS OF COURSE is a wild generalization. It is *my* Manhattan that has kept the same—yours and anyone else's may well change as often as the two Hinkseys. It's all in my mind, my emotions, and perhaps my jet lag!

It is true, though, that with the possible exception of Venice, Manhattan retains its physical character more tenaciously than any other great city of the Western world—partly because it is an island, I suppose. It comes as a genuine shock here when some familiar landmark disappears—not just the usual pang of nostalgia for the past, but a true sense of personal loss.

Stores, restaurants, hotels come and go, of course, but very often Manhattan locations, however drastically they adapt to changing needs or opportunities, keep their personalties anyway. Grand Central Terminal has been revivified, but remains a terrific new version of its beloved old self. The Plaza Hotel is transformed, but thanks to strength of public opinion will apparently remain, like the collapsed campanile at Venice after its rebuilding, *com'era, dov'era*—as it was, where it was. Even Columbus Circle, which has been sensationally rebuilt, still somehow looks to me much as it always did, only more so.

For my Manhattan is a sentimental old body at heart, deeply fond of itself, and thus in many ways doggedly preservative. Out-of-town Americans still think it the very epitome of racy modernity, but to me it has for many years seemed a bit old-fashioned. I went to tea one day in an apartment infinitely more traditional, I swear, than anything in London—where the Earl Grey tea came with scones and cucumber sandwiches, where every inch of occasional table held its exquisite collection of trinketry, amd where the little dachsund who sat with us was visiting, all alone, from the flat next door.

And when, as part of my demi-centennial celebration, I gave a performance at the New York Public Library on Fifth Avenue, my! how like old times it was, how incongruously simple the reception they gave me in that palatial house of learning, the laughter almost rural in its innocence, the welcome so unfeigned—there in the heart of the mighty metropolis, where the yellow cabs streamed by in their hundreds and the fire trucks screamed!

MUCH MORE IMPORTANT than the physical condition of a city, anyway, is its temperamental condition. Now as always, Manhattan is in intermittent frenzy. I have known it in political frenzies, social frenzies, frenzies about soap operas, or baseball games, or sex scandals, or the state of the stock exchange, or the state of the Union. One transient excitement or another dominates conversations in this city as it dominates the news bulletins, and sometimes of course there are several excitements at the same time.

During my celebratory visit these were some of the matters that seem to have preoccupied my acquaintances in Manhattan: soccer (*soccer?*), traffic congestion, gun violence (oh my God!), Iraq (oh my God again!), electoral chances, climate change, racism and rappers, George Bush and Tony Blair and Harry Potter. Give or take a name or two, or an anxiety, they could be the preoccupations of my acquaintances here several decades ago. For ecological threat read nuclear war, for Baghdad read Saigon, for Potter substitute Holden Caulfield, call back Reagan and Mrs. Thatcher, and Marilyn Monroe, and Billy Graham, and Spiro Agnew—in manner and commitment the conversations were much the same, except that in older times they were often conducted over long merry sessions of dry martinis.

In my experience, martinis or no martinis, the discussions have often been passionate, but not often vicious. I have always thought that if I had to have a heart attack somewhere, I would prefer to suffer it somewhere in midtown Manhattan. For all its reputation of cynical glamour, this is a *kind* city. I did fall over once—down in the Financial District, too—and was touched by the generic sympathy of Wall Street as I was helped to my feet, dusted down, and sent on my way with a clutch of clean tissues.

"Take care," said that Ruthenian cabbie as we parted, "mind how you go," and he meant it. Often and again, all down the years, I have been struck by the sincerity that so often informs the clichés of New York social intercourse—the mantra "Have a good day," for instance, which is so often scoffed at in England, is frequently spoken in Manhattan with real meaning. When a doorman at a Borders bookshop said "Enjoy your evening," as I left the store at closing time, it did not sound like a mere throw-away slogan, but a genuine pleasantry between passing acquaintances.

I must not, of course, relapse into sentimentality. The insults and accusations that fly around Manhattan are equally sincere, as any resident will be quick to expostulate. But I write as an outsider, and in my view there are few great cities more courteous to its guests.

■

BUT SOMETHING TELLS me, all the same—remember, this is all in the mind!—that there has been some subtle change to the nature of Manhattan since I first knew it. People tell me the city has never been quite the same since the tragedy of 9/11, and I do seem to sense some sort of coarsening in the air, a loss of composure, perhaps.

The first thing that greeted strangers like me when we sailed into Pier 92 half a century ago, was the romantic waterfront skyline, dominated then by skyscrapers of the 1930s, but irrevocably altered when the twin towers of the World Trade Center went up. I was never keen on those enormous blank obelisks. They seemed to me even then an insensitive bloating of the Manhattan style.

For the island city that had emerged from World War II seemed to me essentially a city of grace, its inevitable urban squalor redeemed for the stranger by a wonderfully civilized civic architecture. Whether they were Art Deco masterpieces like the Chrysler Building, or elegant internationalist examples like Lever House, or even post-modernist exuberances adorned with squiggles and fancy plinths, in those decades the iconic constructions of Manhattan seemed to get on well together. They struck me, in my anthropomorphic naïvety, as a tolerant lot of structures, respectful of their neighbours and fastidious of attitude. They were doubtless built out of greed, but they did not seem greedy. They spoke of tradition as well as innovation, and one could think generically of them as true emblems of humanism.

Plonk, as if they had fallen out of space, in the 1970s came the twin towers, taller and bulkier than anything else, oblivious of their surroundings, impossible to categorize except in terms of sheer bulk. They seemed to me essentially selfish. They heralded the virtuoso arrogance of fashionable twenty-first-century architecture, with its tactics of shock and surprise and its disregard of neighbourhood. They represented ethos rather than art, and their attitude has since swept the world, and is, in my perception, insidiously pervasive in contemporary Manhattan.

For example I stand at my eighty-first-floor hotel window above Central Park, in perfect air-conditioned silence, thinking. I am an impressionist, not an analyst, and at first I cannot make out what is different about the view out there, since I first marvelled at it in my youth. The park is still gloriously green, and the same familiar carriages trundle around it. The grand old buildings that line it retain their scale and discretion, and their windows glitter, and their flags fly as splendidly as ever.

But gradually, as my mental focus clarifies, I seem to discern there a suggestion of ideological change. In the new century buildings have sprouted everywhere among and behind those friends of my lifelong prospect, filling every nook and interstice, elbowing their own space, and they bring to the scene a new sense of *jostle*. Is it just capitalism in its feral fruition? Or does it really represent some profounder metamorphosis of the city spirit? Architecturally many of them are handsome: allegorically they disturb me rather.

"They disturb you!" scoffs the New Yorker who joins me at my window. "They disturb you allegorically! What a load of figurative garbage."

BUT LATER WE had lunch together in a room which, beyond all others, represents for me that old truce-like serenity of Manhattan, from the 1960s and 1970s perhaps, when the harmony of its structures seemed to me representative of decency among its people, and buildings and citizenry seemed equally ready to give me a hand if I collapsed on 42nd Street.

The room was the Four Seasons restaurant, within Mies van der Rohe's bronze-and-glass Seagram Building, his masterpiece of 1958. The building itself is the supreme temple of my Manhattan, expressing most exactly what I most admire about the island city, and the restaurant was designed by the great Philip Johnson to be a cool sanctuary at the core of it. I think of it as the gentle concord of two masterly creative minds, at the apex of a civilization. The Four Seasons is frightfully expensive, but to hell with the cost (to my mind purely figurative, as I told my friend when he paid the bill).

There is a pool in the middle of the lovely room, and the tables are generously spaced. It was all dappled sunshine that day. My companion was a delight, I ate soft-shelled crab, a waiter I knew told me about his recent illness and pointed to The Man Upstairs as the source of his recovery. Altogether I felt, once again, under the influence of the Manhattan genius (plus the crab), that the heart of the old place really did not change, whether in the fact, the fancy or just the sweet desire.

But my host, being a true New Yorker not given to saccharine, reminded me that Philip Johnson and Mies van der Rohe had acrimoniously parted company after their master-work was done. "Allegorical, don't you think?" he snidely suggested.

Travels with an Old Dog

HALF-WAY THROUGH A protracted meander through Europe in 2004, I fell in love with a big black dog. He was very big, very black, very hairy, extremely old, and he slouched among the stalls of a city market, head and tail drooping, with an air of exhausted aristocracy. He looked world-weary, monstrous, immensely experienced, tolerant and faintly amused by life.

At first I did not recognize this marvellous animal, but in retrospect I realized who he was. He was Leonardo da Vinci. He was Lampedusa's Leopard. He was Bismarck's uncle, Philip II in old age, Churchill's after-ego. He was, in short, Old Europe, and if he seemed to be picking his way through the market crowds with fastidious aloofness, that was because the market-place that day was such a jostling muddle.

There was no pretending that Europe at that particular

moment of its history felt logically ordered. Much of it considered itself a union, but my wanderings through its north-west corner took me over five frontiers of decidedly varied character. There was a tunnel under the sea. There was a bridge across an estuary. There was a ferryboat. There was a ship. There were several apparently deserted old customs posts, and the most abandoned of them appeared to be at the frontier of the European Union itself, taking me into Norway, which is not within the union and uses its own currency, out of Sweden, which is within the union but does not use the euro.

No wonder that grand old dog shuffled bemused through the market, and through all the impressions of my stay!

THE FALTERING OF Europe then was a disappointment for those who dreamed of a super-continent to restore the balance of the world, a triumph for those who still believed in the glory of the Nation-State, and a bit of each for those of us (like me) who wanted a confederation of peoples devoted to their own ways and languages, but ready to sacrifice to Caesar those dullard matters of war, finance and foreign affairs that properly belong to emperors.

So for myself I was happy to find national characteristics, if not national sovereignties, still unmistakable. The moment I drove off the Euroshuttle train under the Channel, confident in the miracle of satellite navigation to declare my route for me, I found that road-works in the Pas-de-Calais had disoriented everything. "Never mind," said my companion, "we're in France now—trust the French": and sure enough, simple, clear and highly intelligent

Deviation signs guided us around the diggers and rollers, over temporary bridges, under slip roads, to set us safely on the way to Antwerp and the north. As Sterne discovered all those years ago, they order these matters better in France.

It was the same when we got into Holland, and settled for a night at Zutphen. How exceedingly Dutch it was still! With what maidenly grace the young Dutch ladies rode their very upright bicycles around the town, like so many students at a finishing school! And when, behind the cathedral, we found that a modern commemorative statue of a lion had been recently decapitated by vandals, how wonderfully Netherlandish was the response of the passing citizen who explained the spectacle to us. She was out for an evening stroll, she was as exquisitely made up as if she were off to a wedding, and her attitude was serenely apologetic. "It happens everywhere," she said, surveying the mutilated beast before us, which had various bits gouged out of it, and a regretful bunch of flowers at its base, "but I'm afraid nothing happens quite like it happens in Holland."

In Germany the national characteristics I noticed were my own. We found ourselves spending a night in a prosperous suburb of a decidedly prosperous industrial town, so prosperous that a police car discreetly patrolled its leafy lanes, and hardly a villa was without its double garage, its lawn and its rockery. Nobody I met in this place was in the least disagreeable, but I found myself shamefully resentful of everything I saw. The parked cars looked obscenely rich, the gardens ostentatiously well-tended. There was something baleful to the padded and cushioned calm of it all, as there was to the patrol car swishing gently by, and the most benign of the villas reminded me only of that house beside the Wannsee at Berlin where they drew up their plans for the Final

Solution. I was ashamed of these totally unreasoned reactions, but there we are, I am a child of my times; and as a matter of fact, when I later confessed them to a German ambassador, he said he quite understood.

I had been rashly invited to stop in Sweden to speak at an extremely intellectual seminar about imperialism, and found myself all unexpectedly in a vortex of Swedish capitalism. I had never heard of my patrons before, but they turned out to be sponsors of a foundation behind which there stood, I gradually discerned, a gigantic conglomeration of mercantile and financial enterprise—scores of associated companies, related by family inheritance, with interests in shipping and construction and all kinds of consumerism. My principal hostess bore herself like a queen, and I realized that as one of the most powerful women in all Scandinavia she was used to being treated like one: but this being Sweden, the whole vast concern expressed itself with infinite grace and courtesy, and I was put up in a lovely room in an exquisite old country house, and handsomely fed, and given a book about the conglomerate, and so bluffed my way with impunity through all social and cerebral challenges.

And how's this for a taste of Norway? From the coast south of Oslo the Telemark Canal runs for a hundred miles deep into the mountainous heart of the country, and two antique steamers (the *Victoria* [1882] and the *Henrik Ibsen* [1907]) carry tourists from one end to the other. The voyage takes eleven hours, including the passage of eighteen locks, and passengers disembark at one of Europe's most delightfully weird hotels, in an isolated hamlet at the head of a lake. The building is made of wood, and is turreted and balconied, bobbled and fretted, lace-curtained and stained-glassed, decorated with dragons' heads, equipped with croquet mallets and a Ladies' Lounge. A pianist ornaments the evening hours with Grieg and Cole Porter, and at 8:30 next morning the more indefatigable of the excursionists troop down to the landing-stage for their eleven-hour journey back again, to a toot of the steam-whistle from *Ibsen* or *Victoria*.

IN MY FANCY the dog was present at all these venues. He was first off the *Henrik Ibsen*, looking understandably relieved after those eighteen locks; he was perfectly at home at the seminar; he growled slightly, as in a dream, at the German suburban police car; he sniffed sadly around the plinth of the decapitated Dutch lion; he never for a moment doubted the Deviation signs in the Pas-de-Calais.

But in my mind he really came into his own, assuming an almost heraldic bearing, when in the course of the journey we discovered symptoms of a European presence beyond the wrangles of constitutionalists. For instance he was proud when, entangled mile after mile in a ceaseless progression of trucks around the power centres of Antwerp, Rotterdam and Hamburg, we crossed the Rhine to find that the vast energy of the continent was not only thundering around us on the highway, but was pounding below us too, in the mighty stream of barges making for the sea.

He was pleased by the spectacle of the old Soviet submarine U359, high and dry on the quayside of Nakskov, in Denmark, in reassurance that at least one threat to the meaning of Europe had lost its sinister power. He smiled with approval to find that four empty beer cans, neatly lined up on a sidewalk, were all the rubbish left behind by a rowdy Swedish disco party. He basked in the general sense of shared values, common kindnesses, that gave all these peoples a sense of relationship. He was thrilled by a moment of fulfilment when, beneath a brilliant blue sky, above a waterway speckled with white sails, we soared over the celestial new bridge that connects Danish Copenhagen and Swedish Malmo, cocking an exhilarating snook at the very notion of frontiers between societies.

And yes, in a condescending way (for he is evidently rather old-fashioned in his views) that conceptual dog of Old Europe actually wagged his tail when, having crossed the North Sea on a Norwegian ship, we were greeted in drizzly South Shields with a traditional English welcome. Two burly officials in yellow raincoats stood unsmiling beside the immigration booths, evidently ready for the worst, but when I showed our passports to the man at the desk he simply said: "That's OK, pet. On you go. Sorry about the weather."

The Hero

THANK GOD NELSON died at Trafalgar! Can't you imagine the bathos of the hero in his old age, absurdly vain, increasingly testy and hypochondriac, drinking too much, plastered all over with decorations, forever trying to avoid poor Lucy Nelson and recalling old victories in the arms of his grotesquely obese and fulsome mistress Emma Hamilton?

But then again, thank God for Emma! If there were more Emmas, as the Admiral said himself, there would be more Nelsons, and certainly without her the most operatic of England's national romances (at a Verdian rather than a Wagnerian level) would hardly be a romance at all—just the career of a fighting admiral whose principal merit, so Lord St. Vincent thought, was mere animal courage, and whose lovelife followed a familiar naval pattern of humdrum wedlock punctuated by distant and transient infatuations.

Without Emma's husband Sir William, too, the tale would lose much of its charm. What a thoroughly agreeable old cuckold he was, and what an artistically important part he played in the *ménage à trios*! He was more than just a foil, but a dramatic mirror to the passions of the spectacle, for he loved Emma almost as besottedly as Nelson did, and made the perfect Dr. Watson to Nelson's Sherlock—or, one might perversely say, a Horatio to his Hamlet.

And what would the grand opera be without its chorus? Behind the virtuoso stood his Band of Brothers, worthy understudies one and all, steady bald Hardy, impetuous Berry ("Here comes that damned fool Berry! *Now* we shall have a battle!"), Foley always in the van, Beatty the gentlest of surgeons, "good dear little Parker"—and behind them again the rough, bluff, cosmopolitan company of seamen, half of them distinctly reluctant recruits to the Royal Navy, who threw themselves into Nelson's service with a devotion worthy of football crowds or rock fans, and "cried like wenches" when he died.

The real allure of the scenario lies in its theatrical antithesis between life at sea and life ashore. What a perfect ass the Saviour of Europe could be, when he was away from his ships! How preposterously he swaggered around with his stars and his medals and his sashes and his scarlet pelisse and the *chelengk* on his cocked hat, given him by the Sultan of Turkey, whose diamond centre revolved when you wound it up! And what kind of a hero was it who, receiving a letter from the loving wife he had so shamelessly deserted, sent it back it to her with the despicable inscription "Opened in error. Returned unread." Surely, one wonders, no amount of animal courage, no number of annhilations, could make up for Nelson's failings?

But the glorious denouement of the performance does it. The Duke of Wellington, at his only meeting with Horatio, thought at first what a coxcomb and charlatan he was, only to discover that after a time his conversation became of matchless interest. Never had he known, recalled the Duke, such a complete metamorphosis; and never did caterpillar mutate more marvellously into butterfly than when Nelson the vainglorious landsman turned into Nelson at sea, and set sail for Trafalgar.

Of course we always know it's coming: the swooning farewells from Emma, the adoring crowds on the promenade at Southsea, the dinners with the captains off Cadiz, the touching small kindnesses to midshipmen and sailors, the last letters, the noble prayer before battle, the fatal blaze of decorations on the quarterdeck, the heart-broken officers around the cockpit, Hardy himself, having kissed Nelson goodbye at the admiral's command, kissing him again to show that he meant it. . . .

However often this libretto is worked in the end Nelson always gets us cheering in the aisles. One aria in particular sticks in my own mind, and perhaps reaches the truth about his character. He was, wrote *Victory*'s chaplain Alexander Scott, "the greatest and most simple of men—one of the nicest and most innocent . . . an affectionate, fascinating little fellow."

He remains, I suppose, nearly everyone's romantic ideal of that lost paragon, the true-born Englishman, so brave, so fallible, so bashed about by war, so heedless of precedent or convention, so gloriously sure of himself. Can you imagine him living in our own day, obliged to serve out his time as second in command to some dullard born-again acronym?

Sneezing

TO MOST BODILY evacuations there is, I think, a certain pleasure, if only of relief. I choose my words delicately, but you will
know what I mean. Getting rid of fluids or substances which are
surplus to our requirements, or have fulfilled their purposes,
is generally a satisfying process—as a celebrated Himalayan
climber of my acquaintance put it to me long ago, buttoning up
his trousers as he emerged from a nearby gully, there's nothing
like a good shit.

Actually, though, in my opinion there is nothing like a good
sneeze. Among all these clearances, the sneeze stands alone. Even
its English name owes its derivation, I gather from the *Oxford
Dictionary*, to a mishearing—it used to be *fneeze*. I surmise that
people understandably didn't believe there was such a word, and
gave it an opening *s* instead. Even in its reformed version it was

quite unlike anything else, and so it has always remained a bit of a laugh in itself, vaguely representing the noise a sneeze makes.

In many languages the word for sneezing really is more or less onomatopoeic, which adds to its innate suggestion of comedy. The Serbo-Croats call it *kijati*, the Hungarians *tüsszant*, the Welsh *tisian*, the Fijians *suru* and the Italians *starnutare*. I don't know how all these various verbs conjugate, but I suspect that in any of their languages we might understand that the speaker was talking about sneezing. Even the few hundred people who still speak the Cornish language might just make themselves understood when they apologize for *strewy*. Even the Hawaiian *kihe* must sound, I would imagine, rather like *atishoo*.

For in the common view, at least in the English-sneezing world, *atishoo* is how a sneeze transliterated appears, and I often find that when I sneeze it does sound exactly like that, as if I am acting in amateur dramatics. The sound of a sneeze can be downright majestic, especially if it is one of those convulsions that take a long time to reach fulfilment, keeping everyone in suspense, not least the sneezer, until the moment of explosion arrives. But in general most of us, I suspect, find it rather funny. It goes with red noses and seaside postcard humour. It is a Falstaffian evacuation. There was a time when writers of farce could with impunity make fun of stuttering. No longer, and I have a feeling sneezing may go the same way. Like passing wind, we cannot always help it, but I suspect social custom will make it less and less permissible. It used, after all, to be a stock constituent of music-hall comedy: the stout florid man flourishing his enormous spotted handkerchief across his face in order to catch the effluence of a gigantic sneeze. I have not seen it for years, though—perhaps it went the way of music-halls themselves—and that may be a portent for sneezing itself.

For I fear the sneeze is dated. It is like whistling, or the yo-yo. We seldom see it on the stage nowadays. We seldom hear a frank *atishoo* on the subway. That fat man with the spotted handkerchief seems to be extinct. We have tolerated it because it makes us laugh, but soon it will be politically incorrect to make jokes about it, and socially unacceptable even as an involuntary method of nasal hygiene. So, like the fart, it will wither away in polite society, fainter and fainter in the public memory, to be replaced by evacuative symptoms altogether more discreet, more elegant, and less likely to raise horse-laughs in the stalls.

A Night at the Seaside

A NIGHT AT the opera at Llandudno, on the holiday coast of north Wales! The idea might make Groucho smile, but for most of the world it probably sounds a contradiction in terms, like caviare at Coney Island, say. For most of the world the name of Llandudno goes with dated seaside pleasures, donkeys on the beach, pier-head concert parties, and men with handkerchiefs knotted over their heads, together with the odd party political conference and steamer trips to the Isle of Man.

But I went there once to hear the Welsh National Opera sing *Rigoletto*, and found that Llandudno on the right day can be just Verdi's style.

IN THE FIRST place its setting is almost operatically beautiful. To my mind its topography makes it one of the most surpassingly lovely coastal resorts in Europe, on a par with Opatija on the Adriatic, which was formerly Abbazia, and where the patricians of old Vienna used to flock for their summer holidays. Mountains in a distant ring behind it, a wide bay in front, a high bare hill rising in the very centre of the place, with a tea-garden half-way up and a shimmer of light off the sea—time and again on my visit I was reminded of the garden villas of Opatija, clustering at the water's edge for the gratification of dukes.

Architecturally, too, Llandudno is rather like a stage-set, relatively untouched by modernist notions of theatrical design. The waterfront retains a classic Victorian unity. Its two parallel streets around the bay were built in the mid-nineteenth century more or less at a go, obeying strict precepts of scale and proportion, and they have been miraculously preserved ever since, hotel after hotel along the promenade, shop after shop behind, with glass canopies over their sidewalks. The world expects tatty boarding-houses and run-down once posh hotels, but in fact the whole ensemble is bright with new paint, and looks indeed as though it might all be whisked away on a revolving stage, to make way for Act Two.

For Llandudno's Act One, like Opatija's, was rather grand, and has left its traces to this day. The ancient Mostyn family were its chief patrons as a commercial venture, and gave the project social cachet from the start. It never caught up with Brighton, so close to the English metropolis, but still it attracted diverse swells who have never been forgotten, at least in publicity brochures. Princes and emperors came here, as they went to Abbazia, and there was a time when Llandudno boasted more businesses By Appointment to Royalty than anywhere else in Britain except London. One such visiting swell was Queen Elizabeth of Romania, whose

judgement of the town as a beautiful haven of peace, translated
into Welsh, promptly became the town's official motto.

Think of it! Wartski's the Llandudno jewellers, 93 Mostyn
Street, bought most of the Czar's jewelry when the Bolsheviks
sold it! John Jones along the road supplied Royal Sandringham
Sausages to Queen Victoria! Queen Rambai Barmi of Siam
lived at the Imperial Hotel until, during World War II, she had
to make way for requisitioners of the Inland Revenue! And in
a house called Nantyglyn, 59 Church Walks, for years there
resided the missing last staves of Mozart's Rondo in A Major (K.
386), whose pages had been scattered across Europe since 1791.

Sufficiently operatic? But the second act is still to come.

IT WAS THE railway, in the long run, that turned the reputation
of Llandudno into honky-tonk. It meant that, just as Brighton
became a kind of suburb of London, this town was half-annexed
to Liverpool and Manchester. The railway brought the chorus in.

The holiday crowds of Llandudno are much like British holiday crowds anywhere else. They contain their fair share of the
obese, the yobbish and the raucous. The same thump of rock
music blares from passing cars with shirtless youths in them.
Countless caravans park in their field around the bay, and hundreds of tourist coaches roll in from Merseyside. The outdoor
cafés proliferate with beers, ice-creams and tattoos. If there are
no men with knotted handkerchiefs over their heads, there are
hundreds in baseball caps.

But there is a difference in Llandudno. There is an unexpected wistfulness to its crowds, and this is because so many of

its holiday-makers are old. It is a resort of the elderly. Age takes the edge off the fun of it, and makes the town only intermittently boisterous, with a tinge of the sedate, the regretful, even the tragic perhaps. So many old couples, arm in arm along the promenade—so many elderly folk being helped out of coaches—such a prevalent glint of false teeth and anxiety about lost luggage!

"Keep going, chief!" shouts the young blood cheerfully, stepping from his deafeningly souped-up Mini as a pensioner hobbles by: but is he expressing kindness or mockery? The motley Llandudno chorus is rich in suggestion, ambiguity and anomaly, as an opera ought to be.

IT WAS AN idyllic evening for *Rigoletto*. The theatre was full of happy enthusiasts. The performance seemed to me quite perfect. In the interval helpful neighbours taught me how to extract my plastic spoon out of the ice-cream container, and at the end we spilled out into a twilight as headily romantic as Verdi could have wished, or La Scala or the Met could have provided.

It was very quiet out there—hardly a sound of traffic. Around the wide bay strings of light were shining. Along the promenade people strolled in twos and threes. The pier was a gentle blaze of illumination, and beyond it part of the bare hill was floodlit. There was a murmur of conversation in the air, and a strong suggestion of melody.

A night at the opera! A night in Llandudno! I had a Guinness and a prawn sandwich, and went to bed with "La Donna è Mobile" in my head, interpersed with "Oh, I Do Like to Be beside the Seaside."

Four

As gods and heroes might be

The Cruise of the Geriatrica

IT WAS FOR convalescent reasons that I lately undertook a resolutely up-market Mediterranean cruise, with a Greek classical bias, and since I thought of such a cruise generically as being a kind of packaged ageing process, at first I decided for literary purposes to rename our ship the *Geriatrica*. Later I changed my mind.

It was perfectly true, though, as I had foreseen, that we formed a venerable passenger list, and sunset intimations were soon apparent. Hardly had we left the quay than a charming American Senior Citizen approached me as I stood at the rail, and said that since she heard I wrote books, she thought I might be amused by her favourite quotation from Groucho Marx. "It goes like this," said she. "'Next to a dog, a book is a man's best friend, but inside it's too dark to read anyway.' Isn't that hilarious? I just love it."

I laughed politely, but I could not help thinking that with the passage of time the tale must have lost something in its telling.

Of course the passage of time had to be a preoccupation on board such a ship as ours. "Facing Up to Rheumatism" was one of our first educational lectures, and for myself I felt that the ancient seas through which we passed, seas of glory, seas of fate, seas where young gods fought and heroes died, were themselves allegories of mortality's challenge. "Facing Up to Decay," in fact, might have been a more apposite mantra.

HALF OF US faced up to it cockily. Vivid combinations of lipstick and wrinkle could be observed at the Captain's Gala Dinner. Nautical-looking veterans with binoculars were up at crack of dawn to sail into Istanbul. Loud accents of the English 1950s reverberated over gins and tonics through the Whaleback Bar. Proudly muscular old couples marched their obligatory exercise around the promenade deck (fifteen circuits to the mile) before, having dressed formidably for dinner, they joined their friends for cocktails by the pool.

The other half of us preferred resignation, and more often sat in discreet twos or fours over fruit drinks with flexible straws. They were very likely looking at maps of tomorrow's classical site, or discussing the recent lecture about Theban mosaics. Some of the ladies wore shawls. Few of the gentlemen wore white dinner jackets. Unless there was a bridge game going, they usually went to bed early.

But the odd truth is, the two categories blended. The metallic bray of the Home Counties was subsumed into homelier vernaculars, a generally club-like air prevailed, and when the time came for the fancy-dress dance at the Seafarers' Lounge, it was hard to tell which of my fellow passengers represented Defiance, and which were Resignation. This was because, I gradually came to realize, they were united in toughness, in resolution, and in enthusiasm. They were all there to enjoy themselves, and even the oldest among us, even the ones with Zimmer frames, even the palest convalescents, were out for a good time. They were docile in their obedience to the ship's rules, but it was a willing suspension of liberty.

By Zeus, how terrific was their energy! Nothing dissuaded them. With earnest diligence they listen to the spiel of the tour guide. Like aging gazelles they spring up the tiers of the Epidauros theatre. We see them vivaciously haggling with Anatolian souvenir-sellers, courageously experimenting with the effects of ouzo, returning to the ship loaded down with toys for the grandchildren, talking nineteen to the dozen and ending the day with an enormous multi-course meal in the *Geriatrica*'s dining room, for which they boisterously thank the Filipino waiters like old friends and shipmates (which, after half a lifetime of cruises, many of them are).

BY THE TIME we reached our port of disembarkation, I was quite won over. The sprightly enthusiasm of it all had seduced me: the fertile mix of Carnival and Palm Court, and the determination to make the most of everything. On our last day aboard, that delightful old American lady approached me again. "I knew I'd got that Groucho story wrong. I've been thinking about it all this time, and this is how it should go: 'Outside of a dog, a book is a man's best friend, but inside it's too dark to read anyway.'"

This time I really did laugh. I marvelled that throughout our voyage, in museum, taverna, and Seafarers' Lounge, she had been assidously worrying out that joke: and even as she spoke my eyes strayed to the Sunshine Promenade above her head, where the passengers were seizing their last chance of seaboard exercise around the measured mile.

There they were in silhouette, as those gods and heroes might be on a Grecian vase: the mad sinewy sprinter overtaking everyone, the scholarly couple deep in talk, one or two young bloods from the entertainment staff, an old man bowed over another's wheelchair, several solitary energetic ladies, a few game military men forever arthritically on the march.

I had grown to be proud of them—to be proud of *us!*—and as I laughed at the Groucho story, and admired that living frieze above us, there and then I renamed our ship. The S.S. *Indomitable*, I dubbed her then, and all who sailed in her.

Here's Your Jersey, Boy!

I AM RATHER fond of graffiti, at least in emblematic roles. I like ornamental initials cut in the flanks of ancient statues by poets or conquerors, just as I like being mystified by the extraordinary sort of cyber graffiti which ornament walls, tunnels and railway coaches throughout the Western world. What do they mean? Who does them? When? It's as though some posse of aliens has swept through our streets at dead of night, leaving its weird signatures behind. Anyway, as I say, I am interested in graffiti, and one day not long ago was I particularly struck by one I saw in Trieste.

Trieste is a city with a complex history. It was founded in its present form as a southern seaport of the Austro-Hungarian Empire. It then became part of the Kingdom of Italy. The Nazis declared it an integral part of their Reich. The British and the

Americans occupied it after the Second World War, and Tito's Yugoslavia claimed it, and for a time it was an independent Free Territory under UN auspices. Sixty years ago it went back to Italy again, but it is still rather like a multi-ethnic City-State, in which Latins and Slavs and Teutons have all mingled, and people have been tossed about from one sovereignty to another down the centuries. There are people there who have been governed in their own muddled lifetimes by Austrians, Italians, Germans, Britons, Yugoslavs and Slovenians. You never know, looking at the war memorials of Trieste, which particular army the poor fellows died in the service of, and you certainly can't tell from their names.

The graffito I liked that day reflected this confusing pedigree of allegiances. It was perfectly simple. It just said, in a large white emphatic scrawl on a rubbish bin: FUK NATIONS.

I THINK IT expressed a considered historical opinion, and I sympathized with it because I have myself developed over the years doubts about nationhood. However I don't think that whoever wrote it really meant Nations. I think he meant Nation-States. The Nation-State, so the dictionaries tell me, is an organized political unit, and to my mind that is where trouble begins. The concept of the State muddles and perverts the concept of the nation, and is what has given me my doubts concerning nationhood. It is partly just semantics. I dislike the word "nationalist"; I dislike the ungenerous, niggling, mean sound of it. In my mind it goes with wars and squabbles and prejudices and old historic quarrels best forgotten.

But I am sick to death of nationality, too, and I think it is a dying concept anyway. The earth is becoming just too small for political nationalities. To my mind they will one day seem as absurdly primitive as dynastic wars, or the divine right of kings. In Wales you can play rugby for the country if just *one* of your *grandparents* happened to have been born within its frontiers! Just think. Here comes a likely lad wanting to wear the red jersey for Wales. Born in Oswestry it says on his application form. Oswestry? Oh buzz off, lad, you can't play for Wales, that's five miles the wrong side of the border. Anyway, look at all this here on your form, mother from Finland, grandparents from Mongolia, Chile, Malaysia, father from England? Oh, I'm sorry, son. Hang about though, what's this here? *Your Mam's father was born in Llanelli?* Well, *croeso*, boy, come on in, here's your jersey!

You can change your nationality at the drop of a hat, or the scratch of a notary's pen—one minute you are a Dutchman born and bred, the next minute you're a full-blown Australian! You can be French without speaking a word of French! If you can find the right crooked broker you can probably become a Tahitian, or an Uzbekistani, without going near the place! Nationality is an invented condition, riddled with absurdities, and it is my view that when it comes to nationality, you are what you want to be.

For the moment at least you have to carry a passport issued by some Nation-State, but that is just a matter of form. It is what you feel that really counts. I am told that in the early years of the Israeli State anybody who turned up there and said "I am a Jew," *was* a Jew. I can't think it is still true, but my opinion is that if you feel you're a Jew, or an Arab, or a Japanese, or an American, or a Scot, then in a deeper sense you are one. If I were the dictator of a Welsh Republic, I would decree that anybody who claimed to be Welsh, who shared Welsh values, and would accept Welsh ways, *was* Welsh. Here's your jersey, boy.

█

SO I THINK nationality is inorganic nonsense, referring not to nations, but to Nation-States. Nation, State, race, country— they've all got mixed up, and the confusion has tainted public emotions of loyalty and community. "My country right or wrong," that vulgar American mantra, did not express loyalty to a nation, a people, or even a cause, but simply to a political organism, and that is the sort of thing that gives a bad name to nationalism—even to patriotism.

Genuine patriotism is something nobler. The English, whose patriotism has so often developed into imperialism, have long recognized a profounder relevance to it. It was Edmund Burke who dreamed of an England "not amusing itself with the puppet-show of power, but sympathetic with the adversity or with the happiness of mankind, feeling that nothing in human affairs was foreign to her." And it was one of the most fervent Welsh nationalists, Saunders Lewis, who said that in his view true patriotism was "a generous spirit of love for civilization and tradition and the best things of mankind."

But there is bad to patriotism too, God knows. Dr. Johnson said it was the last refuge of a scoundrel, and of course it often is. Those pipes! Those symbolisms! We're nearly all suckers for it. I was in Berlin some years ago for the two hundredth anniversary of the Brandenburg Gate, a structure which is in itself a triumph of German vainglory, a very fulcrum of nationalism and patriotism and Nation-Stateness, a place of victory parades and plumed pageantries and military triumphs. Of course the celebrations ended with the German national anthem, which we all remember as "Deutschland, Deutschland, Über Alles." I knew very well what the anthem had meant to the Nazis, and I knew what it must still mean to thousands of the Germans there that evening, but nevertheless it brought the tears to my eyes to hear it. It was not just that it is a most beautiful tune, and was played by a string quartet in Haydn's original version of it. It was because, despite myself and all my instincts, I was moved by the power of patriotism. The "Marseillaise" would have done it for me just as well, or "My Country 'Tis of Thee," or "Scotland the Brave!," let alone "Mae Hen Wlad Fy Nhadau—Land of My Fathers."

SUCH ARE THE seductions of patriotism, of nationalism, of the Nation-State, but the nation is a different thing. The word has a different resonance. During Franco's dictatorship in Spain the Basque independence movement was officially proscribed and also belittled, the Government always making out that it was just a small minority craze of nuts and discontents. I was writing a book about the country, and one day I met by chance a Basque activist actually at Guernica, the centre of everything Basque, a place I assumed to be crawling with secret policemen. I asked this man to explain to me, confidentially, what the Basques really did consider themselves to be, and he turned out to be not in the least inhibited. He would first tell me, he said, what the Basques were not: and if he began quietly enough he ended in a bellow that I thought, rather nervously, might be audible in Madrid itself. "We are not a region," he said, "not a group of provinces, not a language, not a folk tradition. We are a NATION, EUZKADI, THE NATION OF THE BASQUES!"

He made the word sound ecclesiastical, or ritual, but what is the true meaning, or purpose, or definition of the nation? I don't think any of us, even that patriot of Guernica, is really sure what a nation is. The *Oxford Dictionary* says it is "an aggregate of persons so closely associated with each other by common descent, language, or history, as to form a distinct race or people." *Chambers Dictionary* suggests an aggregation of people or peoples of one or more cultures, races, etc., organized into a single State, or alternatively a community of persons bound by common descent, language, history, etc., but not constituting a State. *Webster's* American dictionary says it is "a community of people formed of one or more nationalities and possessing a more or less defined territory." The *Macquarie* Australian dictionary says it is "an aggregation of persons of the same ethnic family, speaking the same language." The French historian Ernest Renan defined it as "a group of people united by a mistaken view about the past and a hatred of their neighbours." Disraeli thought the Rich and the Poor formed two separate nations, and London another one. The poet Dryden apparently believed *fish* constituted a nation.

I myself feel that a nation is more than anything an idea. F. Scott Fitzgerald once wrote that France was a nation, England was a country, but America was an idea, and as I see it the American idea really has made a nation out of all the myriad peoples who have settled there. It may be, at the moment anyway, an unlikable State, but it is undeniably a grand nation, because of its idea, which nearly all Americans share, and like to call the American Dream. Consider my own country, Wales. It is not an aggregation of people forming a single State, because it isn't a State. It is not an aggregation of persons who form a distinct race, because we're all multi-ethnic now. It is not a community of people of several nationalities, because in Wales we are all officially British. It is not an aggregation of persons speaking the same language, because we have two. It might perhaps confirm Renan's definition of nationhood, but it is certainly not a fish.

Yet it is, to my mind, an idea—or perhaps an allegory. I dislike all sorts of things about Wales, but what I love about it is *Cymreictod*—Welshness—which is a kind of idea. Gerard Manley Hopkins stopped off at a Welsh house once, and wrote afterwards:

Lovely the woods, waters, meadows, combes, vales,
    All the air things wear that build this world of Wales.

It wasn't just the woods and the waters themselves that enraptured him; it was "all the air things wear" that build the world of Wales.

For me that *is* our Nation. And in my view the preservation of nations is the highest purpose of a State. The Nation-State is a transient device in my opinion, destined to wither away, as Karl Marx thought and the anarchists still do. But at the moment, in our time, it is the only instrument we have to enable a culture, a civilization, a way of life, an Idea to survive.

BUT ANYWAY WE all know really that devotion even to a nation is not enough, and it can be downright evil. Even the *Oxford Dictionary* offers, as another definition of the word, "the peoples of the earth, the population of the earth, collectively," and of course that is the greatest nation of all, humanity itself. You don't have to be elected for membership of it, and you can't be blackballed either. I like to imagine a world in which the things that are rightly Caesar's, like war and foreign policy and higher economics, are left to Caesar, at the centre of things; but the things that are rightly God's, the way we think, and behave, and talk, and believe, and organize our private lives, are left to the nations.

As for the Nation-States, which have done so much evil in their time, and bring out the worst in us still, fuck 'em all.

Americans on a Train

DURING THE IRAQ WAR, in 2003, when I was naïvely trying to determine the condition of America, I went down to the South aboard an Amtrak train, in pursuit of *vox populi*. Everyone talked to me, but during our prolonged conversations, when my mind wandered, my eyes sometimes strayed to the tattered newspapers that lay all about, and thus from time to time I extracted items of what was happening in the America outside our windows.

I generally began with the withering of liberties in America. Nearly everyone I asked felt strongly about that, although a lady from Baltimore was too excited to discuss the issue because she had never been on a train before, and couldn't take her eyes off the landscape. A schoolteacher, on the other hand, felt it in his bones that a politico-military cabal, colluding with what one might call—or would have called, when one was younger—the Establishment, had patently shown—

> *Item: A 74 year old man, suffering from multiple cancers, was executed for murder by lethal injection in Alabama: his victim's son witnessed the execution, and complained that he'd passed away too peacefully.*

—that it was directly behind the Patriot Act of 2001, which, would you believe it, even allowed the spooks to discover what books you had taken out of the public library. Hell, what was wrong with that? demanded a retired realtor. There was a war on, the whole country had to fight it, he'd been in the service himself and he knew what war was like, you didn't go into the ring with kid gloves on. "Look at your own Winston Churchill, look at Margaret Thatcher, d'you suppose they . . . ?"—

> *Item: Letter to the Editor: "Sir, I was in the service and in my view there is no substitute for 90,000 tons of cold-steel US diplomacy."*

I moved on to America's place in the world today. The schoolmaster said that it was truly awful, what had happened to our reputation. The realtor said it was more important to be respected than to be liked—had anyone liked the Romans? The lady from Baltimore said my, Oh my, whatever they say about us, I'm sure there's nowhere more beautiful than this America of ours, and on that all were agreed.

Well now then, said I, what about this same-sex marriage business? On this they all talked at once. It was against the will of the Lord, it was only humanity, my cousin Doreen lived with, I was brought up to believe, I was in the service myself, how would you feel if—

> *Item: Staff-Sgt. Christopher Ward, testifying before an abuse hearing in Iraq, said it was his conception that military intel-*

*ligence was "trying to create an uncomfortable environment to
try to facilitate interrogations."*

—what about the unfortunate children, think what the law-
yers will make out of it, the Bible tells us straight out, sometimes
it's cruel to be kind, oh, just look at those trees out there, don't
they make you think of happier things?

*Item: After 58 years the Gotham Book Mart in Manhattan has
moved to new premises. It will have more room, said its owner,
for its hundreds of thousands of books, belovedly disorganized,
plus Tom the resident cat.*

So we chugged on, deep into the South, and I was none the
wiser about the condition of America when we got to Tennessee.

Marmaladeness

I AM AN Anglo-Welsh hybrid. My chief loyalties are to Wales, but I cherish nevertheless the old traditions of Englishness. They are fast fading now, as the English deliberately discard many of them, and as England becomes ever more multi-ethnic and multicultural. Coffee rivals tea as the national drink, curry is more popular than roast beef, they serve California chardonnay in pubs and for every spectator at a cricket match a hundred are down the road watching the soccer.

Still holding out as a national talisman is Marmalade. I give it a capital *M* because I am not thinking of the sweet sticky stuff served up in plastic packages at freeway cafés, but of the dark tangy marmalade, preferably made of oranges from Spain, which possesses in my mind a figurative quality—Marmaladeness, perhaps. I once saw a film clip of the last of the aristocratic British Prime Ministers, Alec Douglas-Home, eating his breakfast before attending some vital conference, and was almost converted to Toryism by observing bang on the table in front of him, with a spoon in the top, a proudly labelled pot of Cooper's Original Thick Cut Oxford Marmalade.

I myself like marmalade just as much with a dinner beefsteak as I do on a breakfast slice of toast. But then for me it has become as much a symbol as a preserve, and wherever I go in England I scour the marts for good examples. All too often I am offered fancy hybrids or substitutes: orange-and-lemon marmalade, marmalade with whisky or brandy in it, or elder-flower flavouring, jam-like marmalade imported from France, supermarket marmalade with artificial colouring or numerical additives, marmalade more like fruit jelly, Ye Olde Teashoppe Marmalade made in an industrial estate somewhere . . .

But I remember Sir Alec at his breakfast, and I persevere. Sometimes I buy Oxford Marmalade for the sake of its unaltered label. Sometimes I stock up with unpretentious marmalade from Women's Institute stalls. And there is a farm shop on the M6 Motorway to which I make regular pilgrimages because of its range of staunch northern marmalades and wholesome organic products from the Prince of Wales' estates in Cornwall.

Mostly I fail in my quest, and in the end my Welsh half calls me home, away from the princely pots and the Teashoppe muck alike. Happily at certain times of the year, when the oranges from Seville are available, this is no sacrifice, because then the very best Marmalade of all is made in my own house deep in the heart of Wales: so dark, so rich in shred, striking such a perfect balance between the sweet and the sour, the set and the runny, that whenever I eat it (hedonistically with my sausages, austerely with apples), I raise an ironic glass to the other half of me, still searching for the real thing on the English side of the border.

The Poet

IN THE 1950S, when I was writing a book about Oxford, my family and I lived in an eighteenth-century former rectory, a type of housing then becoming increasingly available to the public as the Church of England began to lose its consequence, and moved its clergy into less Trollopian premises. We loved it, so I was delighted one day to come across a lyrical poem concerning old rectories by a clergyman named R. S. Thomas.

I had never heard of him, which was not surprising, because almost nobody else had, either—the poem had just been published in his first collection, *Song at the Year's Turning*. I wrote to him care of his publishers, and asked if he would consider writing out the piece for me, so that it could hang in his own hand on a wall of our own Old Rectory. He did so at once, and his spindly calligraphy has been with me ever since, fading gradually over the years, but still in my imagination radiant with his strange genius.

For a genius Ronald Thomas turned out to be, presently to be recognized as one of the great lyric poets of the twentieth century—in the English language. This is a paradox, because he was also one of the famously iconic defenders of the *Welsh* language, the Welsh culture, the Welsh landscape, and above all, perhaps, the Welsh idea. But thoroughly Welsh though he was himself, he had been brought up to speak English, and had learnt the Welsh language only as a young adult. From first to last he never felt able to express himself poetically in the Cymraeg he so passionately loved and defended.

It was only one of the anomalies and contradictions that complicated his entire life, testing his relationships not only with his country and his fellow citizens, but with his family, his vocation, and even his God.

I GOT TO know him later. When he was already famous he came to be the rector of a small coastal town, Aberdaron, near my own home in Wales, and after his retirement he lived nearby until his death in 2000. It is an impertinence to say so, of a notoriously inexplicable character, but I think I understood him, for like many other Welsh persons, we had both reached the conclusion, or perhaps the device, that we could glimpse the divine in the matter of Wales—not Wales as it is today. but a Wales with its language unthreatened, its landscapes unspoilt, its people serene in their own beliefs and loyalties. It was an old, old dream, embodied in the medieval fancy of "Abercuawg, where the cuckoos sing"—an existential sort of Wales, a virtual Wales of our imagination and our longing.

In our lifetimes Abercuawg has been theatened as never before by the inexorable influx of English settlers from over the border, changing the fabric and the style of Wales day by day, year by year, until before long Abercuawg will be unrecognizable in it. Thomas pulled no punches in his opposition to this tragic progression. His enemies called him intolerant, chauvinist, racist, and hostile publicists printed ogre-like photographs of him, glaring wild-eyed and unkempt out of his cottage door: but he did not care, and he spoke out loud what people like me were generally too cowardly, or too ashamed, to enunciate.

He detested, for instance, the vowel sounds of immigrants from the English Midlands, and so do we. He hated tourism in almost all its forms, together with electric pylons and all manifestations of the game-show-and-celebrity civilization. He believed it was perfectly justifiable to be nasty about the English, if it would make them go away. When he looked through a Welsh window, and declared the beauty outside to be "for the few and chosen," not for the crowd that "dirty the window with their breathing," we know just what he meant.

He never thought of himself as a mystic, because unlike his Welsh predecessors among the Metaphysical poets, he did not claim direct contact with the divine. He was a visionary, certainly, but the outer limit of his vision, I think, was nature, not the God his priesthood required him to serve—he thought of the Almighty as a poet, as a mathematician, and above all as the grand presence of life itself.

COULD ONE WONDER, as he grew old, if his convictions weakened? He married twice—first, for half a century, to a gifted artist who died when he was eighty, secondly to a merry Canadian who cheered and comforted the last five years of his life: some of his last poems were love lyrics of profoundest poignant beauty. But despair, he said, was the prime snare of maturity, and he surely despaired of his own vision as he saw all around him, and far, far beyond, his values crumbling and his faith apparently betrayed.

In his later years he spent more and more time communing with the most accessible of the wild creatures, the birds, and the last time I set eyes upon him he was standing all alone beside our coastal road gazing silently into an adjacent wood, as though communing with the crows and blackbirds in its branches. Tourists driving by, I noticed, stared at him without much interest, or perhaps with a giggle, for he was a strange gaunt figure there. When I got home I wrote a little poem about the encounter, and it turned out to be my own irreverent epitaph to a good man and a great poet:

He stood there like an old idol,
Raised from a stony bed.
The strangers sneered, and would be no wiser,
If ever they read
What he said.
But the birds in the wood understood him,
And shat reverently
And affectionately
On his head.

Bouillottisme

IN MY VIEW, dedicated as I am to the proposition that nothing is only what it seems, many inanimate objects around the house have their own mystiques, inviting us to stroke them (oak beams), fondle them (golf balls), abuse them (recalcitrant can openers), throw them across the kitchen (recaltricant milk cartons), marvel at them (wall clocks controlled by radio waves from distant nuclear establishments), or simply cherish them as dumb friends (almost anything sufficiently old, shabby and no longer manufactured).

No other object, though, possesses the transcendental allure of the hot-water bottle, which combines within itself the primary elements of fire and water, the virtues of comradeship and the reassurance of the ages. The French call it *la bouillotte*, and those homely but resonant syllables suit it well. The hot-water bottle speaks to us out of the earliest of mankind's yearnings—out of the womb itself, one might say—but it also expresses an organic tingle of danger and reproach, for it can scald you if mistreated or get its own back on you by bursting among the bedclothes.

There may be some, of course, who have never experienced the presence of a hot-water bottle. Many more, while perfectly familiar with the fact of the thing, do not begin to grasp the complex inner meanings of this marvellous contrivance, and place it on about the same emblematic level as the corkscrew, say. This, then, is an essay in an unfamiliar literary genre: *Bouillottisme*.

MY OWN FIRST hot-water bottles were of an antique ceramic kind, brown and cream, with a round screw knob in the top. Long ago I graduated to the rubber sort, but even in the most old-fashioned pharmacies this can be hard to buy nowadays in a size and form suitable to serious aficionados like me. All too often it is intended specifically for babies. I don't mind at all that it is infantile in size, but even I am reluctant to go to bed with a bottle dressed up as an Easter bunny or disguised as the cow that jumped over the moon. Like the worldly book buyers who instantly throw away their dust jackets, I deal with this annoyance ruthlessly: with a large pair of scissors I mutilate those rabbit ears, disembowel the cow, and rip off the woollen cover to reveal the minimalist and altogether functional shape of the bottle beneath.

A cold bed is essential for the true understanding of the hot-water bottle, because part of its appeal is masochistic. It is essentially a device for the single sleeper or the lonely traveller. It is like an unaccompanied Bach fugue, whose ordered phrases, part emotional, part mathematical, fall so magically upon the bored silence of the concert hall. All around you, beneath the sheet or duvet, is loveless cold, but in one small patch, beside your thigh perhaps, under your back, on your stomach, soft, yielding and lubricious lies a nucleus of consolation. The colder the rest of the bed, the more humane is that *champ de la bouillotte*. It is reunion after parting, home from distant parts, solvency when you're broke, love in a cold climate.

THE HOT-WATER BOTTLE is not, as is vulgarly supposed, merely an instrument of snugness and security. Irony, menace, surprise, sexiness and humour are all mixed up in its ethos, and to those who really understand it the coziness is incidental.

It is ironic because it thrives upon its opposite—without a cold bed it is useless. It is menacing because it may burst. It is surprising because in its own frigid context it is a kind of anomaly. It is sexy because it is often a substitute for a more human partner. It is so funny that one has only to name it to raise a laugh or a simper. And its true glory is this: that in all these various attributes it is entirely individualistic. How could I write such an essay as this about a can opener, a milk carton, a golf ball, or a clock regulated by nuclear transmissions? I can write about the hot-water bottle because it is, so to speak, entirely its own artifact, *sui generis*, and thus defies a world that is increasingly slavish to conformity.

"You don't mean to say," people often observe to me, "that when you travel you take a hot-water bottle with you?" Proudly, almost arrogantly, I assure them that I sometimes do. It is my modest equivalent of the grander eccentricities our forebears flaunted. It sets me slightly aside, I like to think. It displays my contempt for every kind of trend or fashion, for all lickspittle, copy-cat sycophancies, for all dullard bureaucrats and safety experts, for the whole miserable world of authority and counselling and suitable precaution. It gives me some lingering sense of spirituality. It amuses me. It is one in the eye for pretence and hypocrisy. It distances me at once from the package tour and from the rafting adventure. It makes a free cosmopolitan of me.

Vive la bouillotte! I feel like crying. *Viva la borsa dell'acqua calda! Heil der Wärmflasche!* Up the Hot-Water Bottle! You couldn't say all that about a corkscrew.

Conceptual Travel

I PLANNED TO make a figuratively European journey, and having a taste for symmetry, resolved to travel from the Irish Sea to the Adriatic to make a tenuous connection between two outsider places, so to speak—at one end Gwynedd, on the north-western coast of Wales, equivocally attached to England, at the other end the seaport of Trieste, out on a limb at the north-eastern extremity of Italy.

FEELING A LITTLE like Anna Karenina, through hissings and white steam I boarded a train of the Ffestiniog Railway Company at the old Welsh slate port of Porthmadog. The company was one of the oldest railways in the world, and the engine was one of the oldest working steam locomotives, the Merddin Emrys, built in 1879. This stalwart veteran would haul me away from its terminal beside Bae Ceredigion (Cardigan Bay to the English) into the mountains high above, and hand me over to a neat little railcar of the Conway Valley Railway Company. So I would reach Llandudno Junction, on the other side of the mountains, and there I would join a main-line express to London.

We puffed our way heartily up from the coast, and on the way I experienced a kind of idealized diorama of the matter of Wales. Here are some of the things I saw from my windows that morning: misty mountains, of course, fields speckled with sheep, the odd castle on a rock, herons, slate quarries, woods of oak and fir, buzzards, ancient bridges, rivers placid and torrential, wild hyacinths, slag-heaps, cormorants, ponies, racing sheepdogs and knobbly farmers in cloth caps—all rather stagily displayed as we trundled through the valleys, passes and frequent tunnels.

This was a western frontier land of Europe, far from the centre, and no less telling than what I saw was what I felt that day. The two little railway lines, though catering largely for tourists, still possessed enough workaday reality to remind me that Cymru, the Welsh name for Wales, signifies a comradeship. All along the line local people got on and off, most of them apparently knowing one another, talking voluble Welsh and giving the whole journey a comfortable family feel. This was one of the world's anomalies, still different from anywhere else—despite all the pressures of the age, ethnic and cultural, spiritual, political and historical, still more a society than a State.

On one of the two little trains the ticket-collector invited us to pay our fares twice over, because he had a hungry cat to feed.

The guard on the other turned out to be a grandson of one of my oldest friends in life.

THE SECOND LEG of my journey was less entrancing. It should have been romantic. The train I joined had come from Holyhead, the ferry port for Dublin, and was a late successor to the Irish Mail which had, for generations, carried the Anglo-Irish to and from their estates and imperial duties over the water. What's more it was one of Virgin Rail's Pendolino trains, the sort that lean on curves, and was elegantly modern with frightingly high-tech lavatories. But it was not the train that let me down. It was the route, for once we got into England all was dull.

Dull? England the sceptred isle, England of the kings and the cathedrals and the storied rivers flowing to the sea? Shakespeare's England? Churchill's England? Yes: but all those splendours were out of sight and mind as we swept through the dingy flatlands and run-down railway towns of the Midlands—they were almost beyond my imagination, indeed, as I masticated the Penn State Sour Cream and Chive-Flavoured Pretzels with which Virgin Rail sustains its first-class passengers. This was certainly not the superb island kingdom of legend, and it was only half-cock Europe.

The Pendolino system makes for a gently soothing ride, and I spent the four-hour trip dozily hoping to see something inter-esting outside my windows. I was rather excited by a long line of brightly painted narrow boats, redolent I thought of gypsies and pipe-smoking bargees, until the man in the opposite seat told me they were only for tourist rentals. I noted two despondent-looking swans in an orchard, and half a dozen anglers beneath umbrellas fishing in the drizzle on the banks of ponds. I tried to make sense of the inescapable cyber graffiti, those weird ornamental inscriptions that seem to have been left behind by nocturnal hordes of aliens. But I was scraping the barrel of attention, and presently I succumbed to the lull of the Pendolino, and achieved oblivion instead.

UNTIL, BANG ON time, we arrived at Euston Station, London. By presenting my Euro-ticket at a barrier lyrically called the Elgar Gate I was admitted to a trans-London underground train of the Bakerloo Line. Apart from ethnological changes this seemed to me like a re-enactment of a World War II tube train, but it got me safely through my figurative blitz anyway, and in no time I was showing my passport to the totally uninterested customs officers at Waterloo International.

Smooth as silk, then, the Eurostar glided through the frenetically cyber-graffiti'd purlieus of south London, with occasional glimpses of the Houses of Parliament, and immediately opposite them, in the very heart of the kingdom, that tell-tale triviality of contemporary England, the London Wheel. Next stop Paris! Was this, I wondered, a French train or a British one? I really wasn't sure. Nor was the steward who brought me my sauteed pork in apple and parsley sauce. The food was certainly French, the steward evidently so, but the equipment, the engineers, the system, the ownership? A bit of each, somebody suggested, and about then I began to wonder which country we were in. Were we still within the sceptred isle, or had we, when I wasn't thinking, passed sub-aqueously from the Garden of England to the Pas-de-Calais?

No, a look out of the window showed me cars still driving on the left. I should have known. Once we really were through the Channel Tunnel the train seemed to shift its rhythm, shift its language even, and declare itself unequivocally French. It was as though it felt a new freedom in the air, the liberty of France, the space and the style of it, away from cramped off-shore insularity. The canal barges really were barges now. There were basilicas on hilltops, and I saw a solitary deer bounding in glory across a meticulously ploughed field. No doubt about it, we were in France now—and in Europe!

And sure enough, when I arrived at the Gare du Nord several classic symptoms of European travel displayed themselves. There was a memorial to the thousands of Jews who had been transported in trains from this very terminal into exile or death. There was the endearing old rascal, bless his heart, who lured me into his pirate taxi (his wife knitting in its front seat) and shamelessly overcharged me for my few hundred yards' journey from the Gare du Nord to the Gare de l'Est.

And most symbolically of all, awaiting me there was Train 263 of the Société Nationale des Chemins de Fer Français, bound for Strasbourg, Munich and Vienna: for this was that epitome of European raildom, the Orient Express.

"MUST WE DRESS for dinner, d'you think?" I heard two elderly English ladies hilariously laughing, as they fastidiously surveyed their sleeping accommodation on this fabled mechanism. For it was by no means the fancy Orient Express from London to Venice, beloved of lottery winners, anniversary celebrants and footballers' wives. This was successor to a much older legend, and looked the part: age-worn, weather-beaten, with poky sleeping quarters and unshaven foreigners prowling corridors.

The sleeping-car was Austrian, with a kindly stewardess to look after it, and soon she squeezed into my compartment to welcome me. I had heard the Englishwomen ask where the restaurant car was, so I already knew there wasn't one, but she gave me a slightly melted bar of chocolate, a kiwi fruit and two carrier bags containing towels and cartons of drinking water. Later she sold me a plate of black bread, some Austrian cheeses, and a little bottle of white wine, and very good it was.

Ah, said I to myself as I folded myself into shape to lie down on my bunk and eat my cheese, this is the way to travel! The creaking of the body-work! The passing and repassing of footfalls in the corridor outside my door! The erratic shaking of the old coach, the sudden spurts of speed and inexplicable silent halts—this is the only route, thought I, into the heart of Europe!

For to my mind the core of the continent must always be Vienna. To people like me, born to an imperial aesthetic ourselves, Vienna is still the capital of the Dual Monarchy that once gave half this continent a semblance of unity—cruelly autocratic in the fact, homely in the memory. For us it is still Franz Josef, and *The Man without Qualities*, and *The Good Soldier Svejk*, and Klimt, and the Strausses, and *Jugendstil*, and the parade grounds and yellow barrack blocks that once disciplined so much of Europe.

Oh, and *Gemütlichkeit* too—bags of *Gemütlichkeit*. Inside the Orient Express, the motherly charm of our attendant; outside, trim toy-like houses, and neatly tended woods, and small family swimming-pools, and a lovely snow-white Samoyed on a lawn, watching the train go by. Even the mighty Danube, when we crossed it in the morning somewhere near Enns, was in tamed suburban mode.

An hour late and gasping rather, I fancied, the train pulled into the Westbahnhof at Vienna, down the road from the pomposities of Ringstrasse and Hofburg. I had an hour or two to kill, so after my night in the nostalgic but less than soporific allure of the Orient Express I treated myself to a bath and a martini at the Grand Hotel Wien, before catching my next connection in the evening.

AWAY FROM THE heartland that connection took me, away from Europe absolute towards the outer reaches. Asia began on the outskirts of Vienna, Metternich used to say.

The timetables had decreed that although my journey so far had taken me under the English Channel and through several mountain ranges, I had seen nothing of those organic borderlines. Only shifts in the night beat of the wheels had told me in my slumbers that we had laboured up a mountain gradient or raced down the other side, and Europe being modern Europe, not even the murmur of customs officials marked our passage in the dark from one State to another. It was a sort of virtual travel.

It was the same now. I went to sleep in the wooded suburbs of Vienna, I woke to find myself on a wide plain that might be in another continent. Mitteleuropa was left behind, and as we travelled towards the Mediterranean I felt I was retreating from the penumbra of Franz Josef's empire into altogether different states of being, through cultures Latin, Slav and Magyar, through countrysides decidedly short of *Gemütlichkeit*.

My sleeper was Austrian again, but the train was Italian—Trenitalia's Don Giovanni—and already outside our windows onion domes had given way to campaniles, cosy cottages had become those four-square farms of the lowlands that speak to this day of Roman origins. *Landschaft* was *campagna* now, and when we stopped at Udine I saw silhouetted in profile outside my window, perfectly motionless, lost in thought and a little melancholy, the head of a man straight from the Venetian cinquecento, except for his trendy rimless spectacles.

But the train did not carry me to Venice. At Mestre I turned eastward and found a connection that would take me to my second coastline—or as Metternich might have said, the last coastline of civilization. It was another Italian train, called the Goldoni, and it was bound for Ljubljana, Zagreb and Budapest. I was told it went on to somewhere with a name like Nyiregyhaza, but I didn't believe in that. Anyway, there was hardly anybody on it, and I had my dove-grey compartment all to myself.

First we ambled through the vineyard country of Friuli, which was ablaze with a million dandelions, and then we climbed abruptly into that strange harsh outcrop of the Balkans, the series of ridges collectively known as the Karst—Carso in Italian. This is proper outsider's landscape, scrubby country for foxes and banditti, where the functionaries of Habsburg Europe travelled in fear of their lives and virtues, and the partisans of World War II ambushed Nazis right and left.

It is not remote country—getting rather suburban in places, in fact—but it is strangely suggestive and ambiguous, with its scattered hamlets, its lonely war memorials and its signal boxes far from anywhere. It is like a bitter mirror image, as it were, of my other outsider countryside, far away in amiable Wales. And just as an antique railway had carried me away from the Irish Sea into the genial mountains of the west, so another hoary device would take me from these more unsettling heights down to the Adriatic. When the Goldoni stopped at the frontier station between Italy and Slovenia, I trudged down the long platform, entirely empty but for me and my shadow (for it was midday by now), and found my way to my final connection, the funicular tram that runs from Opicina on the ridge of the Karst to the seaport of Trieste.

The Ferrovia Elettrica Trieste-Opicina was built in 1902. Its wooden trams run precipitously down the face of the Karst to their terminal at sea-level, and for the steepest part are taken in hand by a separate funicular engine. It is a very old-fashioned, well-maintained, polished survivor of a lost Europe, and when my No. 2 Tram drew softly away from the terminal that day, and prepared to plunge over the escarpment, it gave me my first sight of the ocean since I had left Porthmadog behind the Merddin Emrys. There the Adriatic lay below us, blue as blue, with the old port sprawled around its bay. It looked like a City-State, an enclave, silent and serene on the rim of an imaginary continent.

As we tumbled down towards the city I could just see, far away to the east, a line of snow-capped mountains. During my whole journey, Atlantic to Adriatic, I had never seen the Alps before! They made me feel as though my whole trip had been no more than parable, and as a matter of fact by the time we reached sea-level the weather had changed, the skies had blurred, and those celestial alps had faded into hypothesis.

A Bag of Tricks

AS MOST OF us sometimes do, I pined one day for Provence, and I found that even before I left home to write an essay about the place, my mind was full of Provenceness.

There in my subconscious, only waiting to be summoned, were the olive trees and the lizards and the long summer shadows, the rackety cicadas, the wine smells, the sunflowers dipping in their ranks—the poet Mistral, too, and Cézanne forever painting Mont Victoire, and Bardot at Saint-Tropez, and car rallies and *pastis* and garlic and gypsies—the whole bag of tricks subsumed in my mind, since I am of a certain age, by the legendary image of Le Train Bleu, which for a couple of generations between the wars sped its complement of statesmen, stars, aristocrats, thriller writers and ne'er-do-wells through the starlit night to Nice and Monte Carlo.

It often happens that fancies become realities, and so it was when I took the train from London next morning. It was certainly no Blue Train, but Eurostar whisked me directly under the Channel to Provence faster than Anthony Eden or Coco Chanel could ever have dreamed, and in no time at all l found myself in a truly figurative Provençal town. What was it called? I forget now, but it gave me all I wanted for a start.

My hotel was satisfyingly eccentric, replete with velveteen curtains, sacred images on landings and clockwork budgerigars in gilded cages. The shops appeared to specialize in *boxes*, dainty cardboard containers of every size and decorative function. Crystallized raspberries seemed a big thing, too. Citizens with beards were playing extremely slow games of boules in the central square, and for dinner I ate lamb's trotters and tripe, flavoured strongly with thyme, or maybe it was red mullet on a bed of artichokes and pine seeds.

What more could I want? I sat over my coffee that first evening, and thought for a time that my job was done already, between the fact and the fancy. I was wrong, though. Provenceness is an elusive abstraction, scorning fantasy and microcosm alike. As they say in the advertisements, conditions apply.

PROVENCE IS NOT an altogether easy part of the world, in my view. Perhaps it is a bit too emotional for comfort. Although they are almost always delightful in the particular, its people can be brusque in the general—or at the driving wheel. Its weather, which in tourist theory is celestially benign, can burst into blistering heat or tropic downpour, and I prefer to steer clear of the big Provençal cities, which are violently heroic and congested. In that dear little introductory town I bought a white sun-hat embroidered with the letters *OM*, because I fondly thought of it as representing the calm Buddhist mantra *Om Mane Padme Hum*, Hail to the Jewel in the Lotus. It really stands for something much more relevant—Olympique Marseilles, one of the most excitable football clubs in Europe.

Conditions apply, and stress is endemic to Provence, even among its beauties. There is an organization called Les Plus Beaux Villages de France, which offers the visitor an itinerary of matchlessly picturesque country locations. You can follow it if you like all across Provence, but Heaven help you if you do, for to qualify for membership a Plus Beau Village must evidently be totally forbidden to cars, accessible only by appallingly steep labyrinths of sun-baked medieval alleys and infested by thousands of people all too blatantly similar to yourself.

I have evolved my own disciplines for the enjoyment of Provence. I avoid, for instance, all multi-starred, multi-forked or rosetted gourmet establishments. I generally steer clear of the coast. I am never seduced by the theme-parkism that has lately invaded these parts, the 350 Nile Crocodiles of Europe's biggest Crocodilery, all Nougat Factories or Yogurt Distilleries. For me one delightful Provençal outdoor market can stand for all the others, and although it may be civilized to share the pleasures of those old gentlemen at their ball game, I try not to be carried away—it can last almost as long as cricket.

Beware of big festivals! They are ubiquitous in Provence, and although they seem to be riddled with obscure political squabbles, they are almost fatally exuberant. I had never quite got over the festival at Aix-en-Provence a year or two before, and this time

I stumbled into the most high-spirited of them all, the Festival of the Theatre at Avignon. Magicians, clowns, jugglers and living statues filled the streets, choirs sang, trumpeters trumpeted, buskers went from table to table of a thousand cafés, and I found myself a momentary curiosity when footballing youths noticed the *OM* on my hat.

Above all I put out of my mind the social glamour that for so long gave an incomparable sheen to the fable of Provence. It has gone the way of the Blue Train! But still . . . if ever I feel like recapturing something of its lost magic, I try looking in the evening, when the lights are coming on, across the bay of Antibes to the waterfront of Cannes on the other side. How cool and elegant the distant town looks then, how remote seem its publicity feuds, traffic jams, and tabloid absurdities! Coward and Colette might still be strolling over there, with the Astaires perhaps, and the Scott Fitzgeralds, and that very nice fellow the Duke of Angoulême.

FOR IT IS one of the fascinations of this place that Provence has such stunning histories of its own. It has had its kings and prince-bishops and even popes, ruling their own minute or magnificent fiefs. Ancient ranks and traditions have meant a lot around here. In the yard of a small rural hotel in Vaucluse I came across a plaque commemorating, as recently as 1988, a "historic" visit by two local Royal Highnesses, and there are places where one may still hear the Provençal tongue, a language far older than France itself.

It is the *localness* of things that gives Provence its marvellous variety, whether in dukes or cheeses. A night spent in almost any Provençal village is like a night spent in another country. One hill town may unexpectedly sprout bonsai trees; another apparently dedicates its entire existence to the memory of a particular medieval poet. Food is often specific to its neighbourhood, and when an entire village turns out to play boules in the cool of the evening, it seems to me that local conditions most certainly apply. Even the smell of the land is local, depending on its product. If it happens to be lavender-growing country, everything from the soap to the soup will emanate the scent of its harvest, and driving gently though the high lavender fields of the Plateau de Valensole is like drifting through a dream of deep purple.

They tell me that Provence is especially interesting to geologists (not least the innumerable gorges that are for me much the most depressing features of its landscapes). Geographically it certainly offers something of almost everything. Sometimes it suggests to me Oregon, sometimes the Australian Outback, sometimes South American prairies. Those damned gorges are incessantly likened, of course, to Colorado, and some of the mountains tug at my always homesick heart with evocations of Wales.

It is France, though. It is always France. In the dark cathedral of Apt, in the very heart of Provence, not far from the venerated veil of St. Anne the Virgin's mother, a terrible death list reminds us of all the young men who went from this paradise to die for France at Verdun or on the Somme. The French delights are here, but the French tragedies linger too: good or bad, everything is heightened, extenuated or forgiven by the old caress of the South.

WHAT THEN ARE the especial consolations of Provence? For me they are the consolations of doing nothing in particular. I was doing just that the other evening after dinner when a small French boy, perhaps seven or eight years old, emerged all alone from our nearby hotel and threw himself face down on a *chaise-longue* beside the swimming pool. After a moment there he turned over, lay upon his back, let his arms dangle and looked up as in a trance at the evening sky.

He was only seven or eight, but I knew exactly what he was feeling. He was breathing the afternoon happiness of that *chaise-longue*. He was bewitched by the rhythm of the cicadas all around. He was lulled by the ambient perfumes of thyme, rosemary, and possibly banana ice-cream. He had achieved the Provençal nirvana, and when I heard his mother calling from the hotel— *Pierre! Pierre!*—he sprang to his feet in perfect contentment and ran away to Maman.

So did I, in a manner of speaking. Next day I took the Eurostar (*né Le Train Bleu*) home from Provence to Waterloo, and with it came all manner of sweet after-tastes.

Five

Do you see that venerable character?

Growing Old Reluctantly

I AM ENTERING my eighties, and thinking a lot about it. Growing old gracefully, or serenely, or wisely, is the generally preferred denouement to life, especially among those who are not experiencing the process for themselves. But for myself, I know of no compensations for the frailties of senility, the fumble and the forgetfulness, and I am growing very old reluctantly.

This is partly because, having enjoyed the human condition so thoroughly for so long, I hate to see it degenerating in myself—its enthusiasms waning, its strengths declining, its talents withering, its abilities shrinking, even its appetites not what they were. It is partly, of course, because life's range is becoming so limited, so to speak: it's no good contemplating a really big final masterpiece, or planning a wild expedition somewhere, because you can't be sure you have enough time. But I am reluctant to join the ranks of the octogenarians chiefly because I so dislike some of the temperamental symptoms of old age.

■

THREE THINGS IN particular repel me in the behaviour of my peers. First, I detest their generational pride, the pride of period. It is a kind of snobbery, and a particularly pernicious kind. The good old days, the good old days! What crass prejudice it is to imply that people of other age-groups are less perceptive, less gifted, than our own contemporaries. I loathe the smile of superiority that crosses elderly twenty-first-century faces when they hear some familiar sentimental melody of the 1930s—"now that's what I call a *tune!*"—just as I despise the old dogmatists who refuse even to try to understand contemporary art—"what's it meant to *be?*"

With this all too well-known characteristic of old age come more subtle intimations of jealousy, resentment, and other discreditable traits which have been in secret gestation during the long years of innocence and hope. For example, gossip breaks out, the pastime above all of the envious and the disappointed. Don't you know them, those pleasant old ladies, laughing so heartily over a piece of information built around a nugget of malice? Gossip is smiled indulgently upon by senior citizens—"Oh, my dear she's a terrible gossip!" they say of each other with a sort of wry admiration—but often it contains within itself an endemic seed of bile.

And finally there is complacency, the fault of the aged *par excellence.* How often have we heard the old folk not boasting exactly, nothing as crude as that, but happening to mention in conversation the achievements of their own youths, when they captained teams, or pulled off famous contracts, or married immensely handsome first husbands! It is as though the successes of the past are somehow more genuine than those of the present, more worth the remembering—and, incidentally, the mentioning.

MANY OTHER IRRITATING evidences make me reluctant to acknowledge my own generation, but these are the chief. The more I recognize them in others, the more I try to repress them in myself. But age, alas, is age is age. . . . Do you see that venerable character looking along the book shelves there, now and then removing a volume to read a passage, and sometimes smiling in quiet appreciation? Yes, that's me, reluctantly octogenarian, reminding myself of my own works, and thinking how much better we did everything in those days.

Falling Over

THE OTHER DAY I fell over in the street at a seaside resort in Wales. Helpful passers-by took me into a neighbouring department store, where the in-house first-aid team assiduously bandaged, cleaned and disinfected me, and gave me a cup of tea. "Do you often do this kind of thing?" one of them laughed as we parted.

The sad truth is, I do. I have been falling over for years. I have tripped, slid, toppled and collided with lampposts in several continents, often because I am reading a book as I walk, or contemplating a distant skyline, and I carry with me always the scars of a wandering mind.

It wasn't exactly a fall, but it was a lack of proper attention that led to the permanent disfigurement of my left middle finger, when sixty-odd years ago I let the steel hatch of a Sherman tank fall upon it as I was thinking of something else. And I suppose if I had looked properly where I was going I would not have stubbed my left big toe on an iceblock on Mount Everest, so that every five years since 1953 the toe-nail has come off.

More often my mishaps have happened in the middle of cities, sometimes prosaically, sometimes rather spectacularly. Falling over in an icy Edmonton is so commonplace, it seems, that it hardly counts as falling at all, only carelessness, and when I collapsed in a main street there nobody took the slightest notice of my writhing figure in the snow. On the other hand jogging in Los Angeles once I tripped at full speed, and rocketing flat out along the sidewalk between the legs of the pedestrians, satisfactorily astonished one and all.

In my experience three good cities to fall over in are Trieste, Manhattan, and St. Petersburg. I was once walking with a friend across Trieste's Piazza Unità when I tripped on a paving stone, and to entertain my companion lay flat on my back like a stage corpse: the municipal response made me ashamed of myself, for when I opened my eyes again I found that dozens of anxious citizens had swarmed about my recumbent form, murmuring commiserative advice. I once fell over beside the lined-up horse carriages at the southern end of Central Park in New York, and I shall never forget the looming silhouettes of the assembled cab drivers, in their capes and miscellaneous hats, crowding genially over me as I lay in the gutter amid the pungent smell of horse-flesh. And when I tripped and fell in St. Petersburg I was instantly befriended by a retired bomber pilot of the Red Air Force, who took me to his shabby apartment for a restorative wash-and-brush-up before guiding me to a nearby McDonald's for what he assured me would be my kind of coffee.

Generally speaking, people have been sympathetic when I fall over. Sometimes, though, they have thought it more polite not to notice my misadventures, and I was amused by the responses of the shoppers in that store at Wales. The night before, as it happened, I had appeared in a BBC Wales television film, and when passing customers saw me in the hands of the first-aid folk, my blood streaming all over the place, my clothes torn, my face ghastly with pallor, "Enjoyed the programme" was all most of them said, as they proceeded towards the check-out.

That's what I shall say, too, when I fall for the last time.

The Managing Director

TO MY MIND the Managing Director of the London Zoo has in his charge an evil institution.

I don't know who he is, and I dare say that personally he is a most amiable fellow, but he is an ex-officio villain to me because he directs a prison, no more, no less, in which more than eight thousand totally innocent creatures, most of them far from their native habitats, are incarcerated against their will, without trial and with no possibility of parole, for the term of their natural lives. He has had many predecessors, too—the zoo's first bears, emus, kangaroos, llamas, zebras and turtles were first herded into Regent's Park in 1828, and in 1832 an elephant, an alligator and a hundred rattlesnakes were transferred here from the royal menagerie in the Tower of London.

All kinds of penal innovations have been developed on this

cursed ground down the years—the world's first reptile house was here, the first koala bear to live outside Australia grew up imprisoned here, a baby hippopotamus was reared in a cage in 1874, and a polar bear cub soon after World War II (when all the dangerous snakes were decapitated, for safety's sake). Regent's Park has been a Dartmoor to the animal world, or perhaps a Guantánamo Bay.

I suspect the Managing Director recognizes no wickedness in all this. He has evidently not experienced the revelatory flash that occurs when you break through the species barrier, the ancient construction of assumptions, part atavism, part religion, which postulates a fundamental difference of privilege between mankind and the rest of the animal kingdom. He possibly believes, like many Christians, that only human animals possess souls; or perhaps he simply feels, as white racists do about coloured people, that a great organic gulf lies between his own species and all others. I would love to convert him—you know what we zealots are!

The argument that zoos are fun for humans is presumably the basis for the Managing Director's involvement in the business—in the past, at least, "experience of leisure development" was considered a useful qualification for the job: but the idea that any animals, in any circumstances, may properly be subjected to perpetual confinement can surely no longer be condoned by civilized minds. You might as well organize conducted tours of maximum-security jails, or bring back public hangings.

And to claim, as the Managing Director probably would, that zoos are necessary for the survival of endangered species is like saying that the last of the Tasmanian aboriginals, before that unhappy people was made extinct, should have been locked up in England for breeding purposes. The Managing Director would presently come to realize, once I had my hands on him, that all the scientific research in the world, all the alleged benefits to conservation, cannot make up for the imprisonment of a single animal in a zoo.

It is the fact of imprisonment, not its conditions, that makes the London Zoo an incubus of horror in the heart of the city. Sentimentalists like to say that animals born in captivity know nothing else anyway—a horrifically Nazi-like argument. In the London Zoo they produce taped gibbon calls to deceive their captive apes into a few moments of happiness, and they actually employ an animal psychologist to assimilate wild creatures into a life under lock, key and constant scrutiny.

"If an imprisoned animal behaves similarly to the way it does in the wild," this practitioner was once quoted as decreeing, "we can assume a degree of contentment." Assume! The impertinence of it! A few years ago zoo apologists used to claim that animals did not share human emotions such as despair or loneliness. By now even they admit that polar bears can be driven crazy by captivity, and yet that egregious savant dared to suggest that we could "assume" contentment.

The Managing Director would say, no doubt, that a visit to the zoo makes a happily educational outing, and he is abetted by all the subscribers, benefactors and employees of the Royal Zoological Society, by the Royal Society for the Prevention of Cruelty to Animals, which is too purblind and feeble to demand the abolition of zoos, and by any parents insensitive enough to allow their children, licking ice-creams, to stare through the bars, over the ditches or through the prison glass at their helpless fellow creatures.

Just as a concentration camp commandant could not claim that he merely acted under orders, so the Managing Director cannot claim that the state of contemporary society, or the general consensus, or the needs of science, give sanction to his job. But he may not be irredeemable. Few villains are. Perhaps he will see the light one day and recognize that the only proper thing to do with his zoo is to close it down. It will have to linger on for a few years, I suppose, as a kind of hospice for its present poor inmates, until one by one they escape at last into death.

After that there should only be a memorial plaque on the spot, remembering the thousands of animals whose lives have been ruined in this fateful place—and perhaps paying tribute, too, to the very last of all the Managing Directors, the Liberator of Regent's Park.

King of the Beasts

IT IS RAINING hard in Wales as I write. Well, no, it is not actually raining *hard*, it is raining *morosely*, which is much worse, and is plunging us one and all into gloom. Nothing goes right for us these days. We lose all our rugby matches. The postal charges are going up. The sheep are huddled reproachfully in the field outside. The only being that seems to be perfectly settled in his circumstances is my cat Ibsen.

Is the cat Creation's supreme invention? I rather think so. Whether it be one of the bigger models, a Siberian tiger, say, or one of the elegant boutique breeds like an Abyssinian, the feline range provides the perfect complement to any lifestyle. Some people detest all cats, I know, and come out in eczema when one approaches, but the most rabid felinophobe must surely admit that, as books furnish a room, so cats complete any *mis-en-scène*.

Take my Ibsen. He is not Welsh at all, being descended from a long line of Norwegian Forest Cats. Among his ancestors were probably some of those Giant Cats who, as everyone knows, pulled the chariot of the love-goddess Freya through the northern wildernesses of antiquity. He is very large and hairy, kindly intelligent, smells of damp hay and has big feet. He could not possibly be called anything but Ibsen, because if there is one thing more than another that he looks like, it is a feline version of a Norwegian playwright.

Of course being a true aristocrat, he blends limpidly and genially into any background. For centuries his ancestors, expelled from Valhalla with the decline of the old gods, became regular Norwegian farm cats, tough, fierce mousers, mighty breeders. Like old-fashioned human patricians in changing cultures, Ibsen's forebears went back to the bog—losing, I would guess, some subtleties of intellect or expression (he does have a distincly plebeian miaow), but retaining those grand old qualities of resolution and independent loyalty that endeared them to the celestial Freya.

Fifty or sixty years ago, though, connoisseurs of true breeding recognized in the workaday Norwegian farmyard cats some echo of ancient distinction. They were plucked from their humble hunting-grounds, given the lofty honorific of Norwegian Forest Cats, brushed by breeders, displayed at cat shows, neutered and sold for ridiculous prices.

Did they care? Did they hell. By sheer force of character, mysteriously transmuted to their owners, they resisted all preposterous ideas of selective breeding or mutation. Whisked as many of them have been from haystack to villa, they remain unaffected. They don't come in fancy colours. They are seldom dressed up in ribbons. They prefer to be in the yard or the woods, with an occasional dip in a river, if there's one nearby. If they could write, they would certainly be writing majestic stage plays of psychological import.

No, no, I know, not every cat is an Ibsen. But every cat, in my view, however pitifully it has been domesticated, de-clawed, in-bred, emasculated or infantilized, remains in its heart of hearts the animal it always was. A Cat is a Cat is a Cat. The sheep may crouch, the humans may grumble, but the cat, within whatever persona he happened to inhabit, remains nobly impervious to the frivolities of time. If Freya herself, in her fog-horn Wagnerian voice, summoned Ibsen to return to his chariot duties, he might go in the end, but only after a protracted yawn, a stretching of front legs first, back legs afterwards, and an apologetic flick of the whiskers to me.

Ah, California!

I ARRIVED IN California once when a presidential election was seething all over the United States. In California it was an election *sui generis*, because the State is so big, so rich, and so different that national issues here are inextricably entangled with issues peculiar to itself. Feelings, of course, ran high enough on the rivalry for the White House, and I made straight for San Francisco, where a large proportion of the citizenry would undoubtedly like to pelt the incumbent President with rotten eggs. "I hate him, hate him, hate him, HATE HIM," cried a civilized acquaintance of mine at the bar of the Pan-Pacific Hotel, and nobody even looked up.

Still, an almost hallucinatory profusion of local paradoxes and ambiguities swirled around the State that day. For a start the Governor of California was the charismatically macho film actor Arnold Schwarzenegger, and he didn't elucidate matters

by being an almost iconically Republican Governor of a vehe-
mently Democratic State. Then hardly had I arrived there than
the California Supreme Court declared illegal the granting of
licences for single-sex marriages by the glamorously popular
Democratic Mayor of San Francisco. He had started authoriz-
ing them six months before, and since then 3,955 gay couples,
men and women, had pledged their vows at City Hall.

Were the justices right? Of course they were—they were
merely upholding the Constitution. Of course they weren't—
had they no sense of natural justice? They were pandering to
the evangelical Right. They were showing that the law cannot
be flouted even by trendy celebrities. Either way, 7,910 unhappy
citizens were left in a legal limbo. My informant at the Pan-
Pacific was appalled, but Cissie Bonini and Lora Pertie were
philosophical about it, so the *San Francisco Chronicle* told me, as
they hung their matching wedding dresses on their bedroom
wall—said Cissie, thirty-eight, "We'll be married as many times
as we need to for it to be legal."

The plethora of local excitements almost pushed the election
off California's front pages. There had been political scams and
scandals. There had been a fierce debate about the labelling of
canned tuna. There had been endemically Californian argu-
ments about protecting the environment, climate change, whales,
ecosystems, bio-regions and such. All over the State Indian tribes
had been building, wanting to build or vociferously arguing their
right to build gigantic gambling casinos. A couple of high-profile
murder cases had been running well, there were the inevitable forest fires, a prisoner died in Solano State Prison after the
removal of a wisdom tooth, a shark killed a diver, and enigmatic
in the middle of it all was Schwarzenegger.

Ah, California! Sail on, sail on, O ship of this particular State—for my money it's above all upon the American-ness you represent, wise and frivolous, kind and disputatious, on the whole trying so earnestly to be good, that humanity with all its fears, with all its hopes of future years, hangs breathless now.

The Mountaineer

TENZING NORGAY WAS one of the first two men to stand upon the summit of the world—with the New Zealander Edmund Hillary he reached the top of Mount Everest on May 29, 1953, and became for a few years one of the most famous humans alive.

It seems to me that Tenzing possessed to a remarkable degree the quality of allegory. He always *meant* more than he *was*. He was not exactly larger than life, as so many public figures are said to be—if anything it might be said that he was smaller, being a light-footed man of exceptional neatness. I got to know him when I was a reporter with the 1953 expedition, and he was in the prime of his young manhood, and actually seemed to me like a figure of life itself: springy, darting, always eager, never apparently tired.

I did not know just how symbolical he was to become, but now I discern three allegorical themes to the story of Tenzing Norgay.

IN 1953 HE was already the most distinguished of the Sherpas, the people living in the high mountain valleys around Everest who had become celebrated as the indomitable high-altitude porters of Himalayan climbing. Tenzing was, so to speak, an aristocrat among aristocrats: he did not climb simply for the money, like most of his peers, but was impelled by the classic mountaineering urge to reach the top of a hill just because it was there.

This was an allegory in itself. Tenzing was the son of an itinerant yak-herder in the south-eastern valleys of Tibet, and was probably born in a tent. And if this almost mythologically underprivileged origin was not enough, even when as a young man he had moved to the marginally more comfortable Sherpa country, he was considered a second-class citizen as an immigrant from the north—not quite the real thing to the intensely class-conscious Sherpas.

Yet already, when I first met him half a century ago, he had become a prince among them, a star and a cynosure. He had reached this eminence by force of personality, by extreme professionalism, and by exceptional responsiveness to the world at large. He had mixed easily with foreigners—Britons, Swiss, Frenchmen, Americans—and readily adopted some of their ways. Although when I first knew him he had never been out of the Indian subcontinent and had never seen the sea, he was already a true cosmopolitan.

SUCH WAS THE original allegory of Tenzing—this fable-like emergence from the stony wastes of Tibet, where the yak herds roamed, to a status of honour among his own people and among the foreigners who met him. The second allegory is, of course, the arrival of glory. A kind of apotheosis befell Tenzing when he reached the top of Everest. It was as though a halo had settled upon him. He became not merely the most famous of all mountaineers, but one of the most famous of all adventurers, up there with the great explorers of the past.

He was a man out of another world, the new world of a renascent Asia. He dined with kings and princes. He was honoured with medals. He rode above the petty jealousies, personal and political, which beset him the moment he returned from the mountain, and he seemed to face the world at large with a grand serenity. Nobody had met anyone quite like him before. Wherever he went in those years of his blazing fame he was treated as a being fabulous in himself—like a unicorn perhaps, or some elegant creature of the high snows.

I dare say there will never be quite such a phenomenon again. Brilliant people out of Asia are commonplace now, and Himalayan valleys do not seem so remote as they did half a century ago. Then Tenzing seemed to most people *sui generis*, and I shall never forget the old English gentleman who, observing Tenzing in the full flush of splendour at an official banquet in London, remarked to me how good it was to see that Mr. Tenzing knew a decent claret when he had one.

YET IN ALLEGORY as in all else, pride really does precede a fall. Tenzing never fell from grace, or perhaps from pride either, but the last part of his life was a story of decline. Perhaps it was inevitable. Age crept in, of course, weakening the feline grace of his physique, and with it came ill health. His family affairs grew unhappily complex. His fame began to fade, and with it his confidence. In his last years he was plagued by depression—the very last condition I would ever have foretold for him.

But here is that third, last allegory. In all his years of hardship and success, of magnificent strength and debilitating old age, happiness and disillusion, Tenzing seems to have remained essentially himself. He seldom let himself down. He looked fortune and history in the eye, and remained a man for a' that. I prefer to remember him always as I saw him fifty-odd years ago, when in the aftermath of his great climb we met by chance near a yak herder's hut in the lee of Everest. I was on my way home. He was going to a neighbouring village to see his aged mother, and tell her the news of the ascent. We had breakfast together beside one of the clear streams that came rushing out of the Khumbu glacier.

He really was like some legendary mountain creature then— brown as a nut, supple as a willow, and when he stripped to the waist to wash himself in the icy water of the stream, how slim and sinewy he looked as he grinned at me through his shivers, rather like a deer that had come splashing out of the shallows, and was shaking the water from its antlers!

I did not expect ever to meet him again, having no notion of the astonishments to come, so he gave me a souvenir of our association. It was a photograph of him, squatting in an open-necked shirt beside a litter of Tibetan terriers given him, he told me, by the Dalai Lama. I asked him to sign it for me, so then and there he did—just the one word, TENZING.

It was a kingly sort of signature, I thought. It was the only word he could write.

Riding the Icon

"ICON" HAS BECOME a cliché word of our times. It long ago
lost its religious connotation, at least in the populist West, and
is applied nowadays not just to the computer symbols that first
propelled it into the popular vernacular, but to footballers, buildings, trendy restaurants or yeast extracts. Not long ago I took a
ride on a train called the California Zephyr, which had once been
an icon itself. I did it for old times' sake, because I remembered
with pleasure and affection my first journey on it, fifty years
before when this Flagship of the Western Railroads was all glitter, speed, assurance and marvellous competence. The Zephyr
had seemed to me then a very emblem of our achievement—of
our civilization, even, up there with the art and the philosophy.

Those confident old times had passed, though, and the
twenty-first-century Zephyr aroused very different emotions in

me. This time I found it more dispiriting than inspiring. Gone was that colossal assurance, the dazzle and infectious exuberance. Nothing worked the way it used to, everything seemed past its best. The train crew had evidently lost their famous railwaymen's pride. The passengers were a great deal fatter. We travelled slowly, and several hours late.

But as we plodded heavily over the Rockies, rattling rather and sometimes subjected to a half-audible commentary over the public address system, it occurred to me that after all the Zephyr was still as emblematic of its time as it had been half a century earlier. Now it just as faithfully represented a world that had grown too old for itself, too tired, too obese, too complacent, too disillusioned. If (as I began to think) it was time for the Flagship of the Western Railroads to give up the struggle, that might be true of our civilization, too—or of our planet. Maybe, as the sandwich-board Cassandras had for so long been telling us, the end of the world was nigh.

HIGH TIME TOO, I grumbled to myself that evening, when the bunk in my sleeper gave way beneath me, and an attendant had to prop it up with packing-cases borrowed from the restaurant car. "Is it always like this?" I had asked him earlier, apropos of the Zephyr's more general sense of collapse. He grinned. "It don't always start like this," he said cheerfully, mopping his brow, "but it don't take them but a minute to *get* it like this." If the prophets are right, and the end really is nigh, it will be easy to blame our own generations of humans for hastening it. Our predecessors were not much better, but we're the ones who have taken the world so close to despair. Wars, ethnic cleansings, perfections of cruelty, degradations of every kind, terrorism, greed and avarice unlimited, vulgarity uninhibited, jealous nationalisms, religious bigotry—all these evils, Nemesis may declare, were released upon the world in their most pernicious and conclusive kinds by the class of—well, let us just say your classes and mine.

And yet, I thought, as the chuckling attendant left me to my slumber, still if ever a final reckoning is made perhaps we shall not be judged entirely harshly. If on the face of it our contribution to eternal history has been distressing, there's been good to it, too. Even some of our innovative horrors—suicide bombings, for instance—have often been impelled by true virtues of courage and loyalty. If we accuse our contemporaries of random savagery, as they kill innocent bystanders along with the targets of their passions, what must we say of our own forebears who, when fighting causes they too believed to be just, massacred whole peoples with their bomb loads?

Other things we have given the world, you and I, seem to me equivocal gifts. I am not at all sure if feminism, one of our most fateful movements, will eventually be judged a blessing or a curse—so noble a cause, so often blemished its execution. Our particular contributions to music, that most celestial of human inventions, seem to me ambiguous: have the gods our judges swayed to our rock and roll, or blocked their ears to it— thrilled to our atonal discords, or pined for another Mozart? Will political correctness, the discrediting of patriotism, the decline of organized religion, be marked up on the eternal record as pluses or minuses? We cannot know. Only time will tell—if time survives.

This much, though, I swear we can be certain of: that ours will be registered as a period of new compassion. God knows many of us have been murdered, burnt or raped—some of us have done the murdering and the raping—but just as many have surveyed the human condition with a profounder understanding than ever our ancestors did. We have known more about the condition, of course, almost every one of us having vicariously experienced its worst miseries on television: but still, can you imagine our great-grandparents turning out in young multitudes to protest public wrongs or injustices, or giving money so generously to help impoverished foreigners far away, or even volunteering in their thousands to try and help in the parched and sorry places of the earth? Genuine sympathy has grown among our peoples, in our time, and a profounder empathy too.

We are more thoughtful about the beasts than our predecessors were. Even zoos were considered in most of our childhoods institutions of entertainment; now they can generally only be justified as trustees of our fellow species. Vast and profitable works of engineering have been diverted or aborted because they might have interfered with the webs of rare spiders, disturbed the residences of small owls, or simply threatened the general eco-balance somewhere. Only cranks and Oscar Wilde once spoke out against hunting: now you are socially suspect if you threaten to shoot some of the bloody squirrels.

We care more for our countrysides, when we are not trying to make too much money out of them. We take better care of our heritage, when we are not demeaning it for tourism. There are still many people in this world who would flock to see an execution, but in dozens of countries capital punishment is now outlawed—a sign of public sensitivity inconceivable a couple of generations ago.

You may laugh, but I think ours will also be remembered, if it is remembered at all, as an age of beauty. There may be fewer sublime artistic geniuses than there were in earth's supreme creative periods, and perhaps more artistic charlatans, but to my mind there is a more general diffusion of beauty. Ours has been a time of fine (if shamelessly selfish) architecture, freeing itself from the graceless restraints of modernism and brutalism and flowering in forms fanciful and varied—pyramids, globules, asymmetrical devices and magnificently virtuoso displays of construction which have sprung up across the hemispheres, and tempered our unconscious responses. For every privileged art lover who made a pilgrimage to see the *Mona Lisa* a century ago, a million tourists and business travellers of our time have been uplifted willy-nilly by Sydney Opera House or the airport at Barcelona.

Domestic design too, in the age of aerodynamics, plastics and electronics, has brought new elegance into all our lives, everywhere. The weapons of war (ships and aircraft apart) are still appropriately ugly—could anything look nastier than a tank, more ungainly than a Kalashnikov?—but the instruments of peace are unprecedentedly graceful. Sold in the most squalid backstreets, clutched in the grubbiest hands, used for the most disreputable of purposes, nevertheless the neat little mobile telephone gleams everywhere like a jewel. The cheapest car can be lovely to look at nowadays, the coffee machine has blossomed into shapes to rival its aromas, and Yves Saint Laurent himself once told me that all I needed to dress stylishly was a simple frock, a raincoat and a pair of jeans—such was the progress in taste since the stuffy crinolines and feather boas of previous centuries.

So at least we of our generations have given to a distracted world a new instinct for simplicity. Our clothes are simpler, our manners are simpler, we do without the richer sauces that gourmands used to think essential to high cuisine. Many a pretentious convention has been mocked into disuse—even members of the British royal family have deliberately made fools of themselves on TV—and formality is generally out of style, together with pomp, circumstance, neckties and protocol.

We have perpetrated dreadful things, we eldest sons and daughters of the cyber age, but if any of us are to be remembered after Doomsday, perhaps we shall be allowed some benefit of the divine doubt. We were murderers, racists and vulgarians, but we simplified the look of life, we did away with some of its cruelties, we evened out some of its discrepancies, we tried hard to preserve its merits, and on the whole we loved our cats.

AH YES, YOU may say, "on the whole." There's the rub. Not all of us, by any means, have contributed to these benefits. Not one of us has contributed to them all. In vast slabs of the planet, in every stage of political or economic development, whether democratic or despotic, violently rich or pathetically poor, humanity has made no moral or even aesthetic progress in our time, but has only confirmed the sceptic's opinion that life on this planet must be nasty, brutish and short. Horrors of every kind, every day, everywhere, big and small, tragic and trivial, belie the very notion of human improvement, and can tempt even the most sanguine traveller, trying to prop up a bed in a railway sleeper, to think the end must surely be getting nigher.

But generalization is the soul of philosophy, as it is of journalism, and it is my opinion that if there are more odious people in the world at this late stage of its development, there are more decent people, too. For what we have given to the world, you and I and all our classmates, is a large, separate, inchoate, unrecognized community of our own. It is distributed throughout the globe, beyond sect or dogma, beyond nationalism, beyond chauvinism—a community of all kinds and races, people old and young, plain and beautiful, learned and unlettered, sharing elements of humour as of taste, and generally recognizing one another by instinct when they meet.

I like to think that I am a citizen of that conceptual nation. So was that merry black sleeper attendant on the California Zephyr, and so I trust will be the dedicated preservationists who, if the end doesn't come just yet after all, will one day restore the Zephyr itself to iconic glory.

In the Land of the Long White Cloud

NOTHING SO CONCENTRATES the spirit of a place as the death of a local hero, and as it happens I arrived in Auckland just as its pre-eminent home-bred champion, Sir Edmund Hillary of Everest, was laid to honoured rest in this city.

It is not the capital of New Zealand, but it is the country's biggest, richest and most impulsive metropolis—its New York, as it were, to Wellington's Washington—and so it is a proper enough place to spend a few days contemplating the Land of the Long White Cloud. The hero of Auckland was the hero of all New Zealand too, and during my stay the story of his life and death filled the sentiments of every Kiwi.

At first I thought all was honest simplicity, governed by the very same principles that had ruled the conduct of Hillary him- self, who began life as an Auckland bee-keeper and rose through a sort of innocently resolute decency to die a Knight of the Garter. But presently it dawned upon me that the Long White Cloud, like every other cloud, contains its drizzle.

HILLARY'S STATE FUNERAL, in St. Mary's church, was a model of decorous pomp. There were none of the tossing black-plumed hearse-horses I associate with such events, but there was any amount of slow marching and ecclesiastical ritual—pews full of bigwigs, a prime minister, a bishop, impeccably pressed uniforms, Bach, a Scottish piper and many visiting celebrities. The tributes were long and eloquent. The organ appropriately thundered, and eventually the coffin was conveyed slowly across the city to be cremated. Everyone was moved, and I thought that in a way this ceremonial immolation of the old champion set a seal upon the nationhood of New Zealand—for so long the dependency of a mother country far away, and still so often overshadowed by its bold and brassy Australian neighbour.

For on the whole, bold and brassy Auckland isn't. In many ways it strikes me as homely still, still recognizably British in its origins—like Hillary himself, from sound and steady stock. Smile at people in the street, and they are sure to smile back. Ask the way somewhere, and you may well find yourself sharing a cup of coffee over a street map. Children are amazingly well-behaved, streets are wonderfully clean, great green trees are everywhere, suburbs are prosperously unpretentious, public transport is splendid, and a benevolent provincial restraint seems to characterize the populace. "If you are displeased with the dining experience," my Auckland restaurant guide advises me, "it is up to you to calmly and politely articulate that to the waiter . . ."

Although young bravos regularly sky-dive from the high galleries of Auckland's Sky Tower (the tallest structure in the Southern hemisphere), and although there are more pleasure boats berthed at Auckland than anywhere else in the universe, and sixteen hundred gaming machines at the Sky City casino, still nobody could call this a *racy* sort of place. Those sky-divers pay $195 each for the eleven-second experience, and are buckled, strapped and supervised safe as houses.

Bourgeois, then, conventional and a bit bland perhaps, is Auckland, but also kind, generous, brave and unassuming: these are the qualities that I imagined sealed in the New Zealand character by the symbolisms of Ed Hillary's funeral.

THERE IS MORE to this place than simplicity, though. I took a ferry to one of the islands of Auckland Bay, half an hour's voyage into the wide Houraki Gulf, and found it to be less like the Isle of Wight, say, than one of the flashier holiday islets of the Mediterranean. Long lines of cars are parked on the roads away from the ferry pier, awaiting the return of commuters from their city offices, and the island is speckled all over with showy and expensively Desirable Properties. It is famous for its wines. Among the vineyards many a restaurant urbanely flourishes, while hedonist trippers like me drink sauvignon blanc and eat red snapper all the livelong day.

Familial respectability scarcely governs the style of the Auckland suburbs, either. Among them you will find whole thoroughfares of trendy indulgence, coffee shops and restaurants and boutiques and clubs, outside whose premises, night and day, the more worldly Aucklanders sit in their hundreds drinking coffee—for tea, which used to be the Kiwi staple, has been so inexorably supplanted by coffee that nowadays Aucklanders like to claim their espressos and lattes to be the very best in the world. Unimpeachable informants (i.e., people I sit next to in buses, or opposite at dinner-tables) assure me that with the coffee, the clubs and the TV all the modern world's corrosions—dishonesty, juvenile deliquence, teen-age prostitution, racial tension, mob violence—have crept into this old Elysium as they have everywhere else on earth.

And whittling away at the old mores of the place, the inherited British standards that tempered dullness with decency, is the jostling multitude of Fijians, Indians, Japanese, Chinese and for all I know Tahitians, who have brought with them both a new excitement and a new sense of dislocation. At the funeral the other day the congregation was almost entirely European, except for visiting diplomats and Sherpa guests: but the crowds that lined the streets outside were of countless origins, and the most touching of the musical farewells was a Maori haka, sung by a fierce choir outside the church doors.

Haka? What's a haka? I'm still not exactly sure, but the indigenous Maori culture is deeply ingrained here. If you don't know what a haka is, or a *pakeha*, or what a *pohutukawa* looks like, bits of the daily press will be a mystery to you, and for my tastes this adds a potent element of romance to society. The songs and dances of the haka, like the fearful battle-cries of New Zealand rugby players, leaven the ordinariness of things with exotic suggestion.

YET BEHIND OR below the multi-ethnic, intercultural New Zealand, and the archetypal New Zealand of healthy middle-class loyalties, there is inevitably a subtle deposit of the homesteaders. Auckland doesn't seem too keen on its original European settlers, but in the days of sail it took guts and imagination to emigrate twelve thousand miles across the globe, robust fellowship to create a new nation, and a spirit of boisterous enterprise lingers still.

Ed Hillary was its very exemplar, but you might not have known it from the solemn decorum of his funeral. When at last the coffin left St. Mary's for its stately journey to the crematorium, we in the congregation were left to sit in reverent silence, and a mad impulse arose in me to stand up and burst into the pub song "For He's a Jolly Good Fellow." What a moment that would have been—the proudest moment of my life—the amazed fellow mourners, bishop, prime ministers, ambassadors, and all gradually joining in, tentatively at first, hilariously in the end, until the startled organist summoned the nerve to add a joyous diapason!

When I mentioned the impulse afterwards all, without exception, said they wished I had obeyed it. But not being a Kiwi myself, whether Maori, Malaysian, Polynesian, old-school British or bravo pioneer, I chickened out.

A Bridge to Everywhere

SOMETIMES I PREFER my allegories explicit. Now and then I don't want to have to puzzle them out. I want them self-evident, and in this kind I particularly cherish a bridge over the motor road E18 at Ås, some twenty miles south of Oslo, in Norway. It is not one of your great bridges. It is only a foot-bridge, in fact, about four hundred feet long, going nowhere in particular but beloved of boys with bikes because of its steep inclines. It is, however, extremely beautiful. A sweeping airy structure of pine, teak and stainless steel, its path is supported by complex parabolic piers that gives it a majesty far beyond its size—an allegorical majesty, in fact.

There is a café nearby, and from its terrace you may contemplate the curious allure of the thing, so modest and yet so suggestively massive, so timeless of feel, standing there in open country with no evident purpose, as though it has been floated out of the empyrean by helicopter, or more properly by silent balloon, and indeed looking rather like some exquisite species of insect. What is it for? you may wonder. Why is it there?

It seems an enigmatic masterpiece, but actually its meanings are simple. It was erected in 2001 by the Norwegian artist Vebjørn Sand, but it is really the creation of Leonardo da Vinci, who originally designed it on a far grander scale five hundred years ago, but never saw it built. So it represents, on one level, that grandest of continuities, the continuity of genius, which miraculously retains its vigour from one age to another.

In the first years of the sixteenth century the Sultan Bayazit II of Turkey ("The Mystic") conceived the idea of spanning the Golden Horn in Constantinople by a bridge from Stamboul to Galata. Hearing of this ambition, da Vinci promptly offered to build for him the longest bridge in the world, 1,080 feet from end to end, 72 feet wide, and high enough to allow the passage of ships. "I have heard," he told the Sultan, "that no man can be found capable of it. I, your servant, know how."

Leonardo drew at least one working sketch for the structure, and though the project came to nothing, and the Golden Horn remained unbridged until 1845, this sketch survived. Five centuries later Sand resurrected it at Ås, and his miniature masterpiece demonstrates that great art and engineering can never seem out of date—for the bridge looks as though it was devised on some virtuoso's drawing-board the day before yesterday.

But Vebjørn Sand had a profounder allegory in mind, too. He saw da Vinci's design not simply as a bridge for the Sultan, but as a tangible image of The Bridge, in the abstract. His bridge crosses no Golden Horn, after all. It stands alone on the plain there, far from a river or a gorge, taking only a few sightseers and harumscarum bikers over the not terribly busy road below. But the absence of practical purpose, the mere representation of an idea, gives Sand's visionary project extra metaphorical power. He wanted not only to unite past with present, but also to remind the world that technology is at its best when it is informed with a sense of the transcendental. He saw his and da Vinci's bridge as "a meeting between heaven and earth, between the spiritual and the material realms."

I cannot help wondering if old da Vinci thought of his Stamboul bridge in such terms—he was also an enthusiastic designer of war machines. As I sit there with my coffee, though, contemplating the meanings of the bridge, I warm to Sand's last symbolism. He sees The Bridge itself as a sort of logo for all the nations, and he wants the da Vinci design to be copied all over the world, in every continent, built in local materials and expressing local traditions.

Perhaps it will never happen, but his little bridge over the E18, where the bikers play, really does seem to me to express a universal hope. No doubt in its original version, if it had ever been built, the brazen armies of the Sultan would have marched over it towards the conquest of the world, but in its cut-down version nothing could look less aggressive. It is an allegory of humanity's better whole. It is at once a bridge and The Bridge, bigger than itself, but no less beautiful.

And when I pay my check, drive away towards Stockholm and see for the last time in my driving mirror the gracefully retreating insect form of The Bridge at Ås, what I like best about it is this: that it goes from nowhere to nowhere, which is to say, from everywhere to everywhere else.

Sex and All That

IN 2012 THE Church of England, a world-wide Protestant sect
of Christianity owing allegiance to the Archbishop of Canter-
bury, was hopelessly embroiled in controversy about the meaning
of marriage, because many members of the homosexual community, male and female, wanted to have weddings in church.
Dispute raged among the Anglican divines, meeting from time
to time in holy synod, over the notion of men marrying men,
and women women, in the sight of God in a consecrated place.

I know nothing about Christian doctrine, and care even less,
but this esoteric dispute incited me to write a letter to the editor
of *The Times*, whose columns had been full of the affair. Could
anybody guide me, I wondered, to any religious movement that
would marry me and my cat Ibsen?

I was not joking. I was genuinely perplexed, as I still am, at the absurdities of organized religion, and its insistence that, if there is such a thing as God, the divine blessing can be categorized. Why should my affection for an animal, any less than my affection for a human being, not be worthy of celestial approval? And why, for that matter, should love between men, or love between women, be less sanctifiable than any other amatory arrangement?

Because of sex, that's why.

IT SEEMS TO me that sex is at once a blessing, a necessity, and a bore. A blessing, of course, because it gives us all pleasure, a necessity because the maintenance of life depends upon it, and a crashing bore because one simply cannot evade the subject of it. It pervades everything, from theological debate to stand-up humour, and every year it seems to grasp a younger generation, so that mere infants are paraded in beauty contests, lipsticked and befeathered, or figure in crimes of erotic passion at juvenile courts.

Mind you, in a way the younger the better, because future generations may tire of the obsession sooner. It really should not dominate the thinking of mature grown-ups. The biological necessity of procreation, after all, is fulfilled long before middle age, and sex should no longer occupy the minds of clergymen or TV audiences. Grow up! Rape apart, the matter of sex is really irrelevant to civil affairs, and one of these days must surely bow out of the comedic repertoire of adults, too. When we are children, we may reasonably find humour in poo or penis, bums or tits, but, dear God, after 9:00 p.m. on Channel 101 we should do away with childish things.

For the truth is, I believe, that sex is a mere appendage to love, and a minor, purely practical appendage at that. Nature devised it as a means of reproduction, added pleasure to it as an inducement, and attached it to affection as a convenient vehicle—for in my view the grand, majestic, infallible, eternal abstraction of love must surely have taken precedence in the order of creation.

SO WHY, I cry, should the matter of sex be of more importance to the clergymen than the matter of love? "You must believe in God," as the Oxford divine Benjamin Jowett used to say, "despite what the clergymen tell you," and he was right there, if there is a God. What nonsense—what impertinence!—that they should value a mere physical mechanism above the ultimate emotion!

Of course it is not so long since many of them thought mere miscegenation (by which they meant the union of humans of different colour) was not only a crime but actually a mortal sin. Most of them have progressed since then. Nowadays only the most bigoted of Anglican theorists would balk at the idea of black people marrying white people, so perhaps before long the synod will even recognize holiness in relationships between species. Then God's blessing might fall upon the love between a donkey and a giraffe, say, or a slug and a mosquito, or a tiger and an ostrich, or even, a bit late in the day, upon my old cat Ibsen and me.

On Whistling

ONE NIGHT DURING World War II, on leave in London, I penetrated the blackout to see a show at the London Hippodrome called *The Lisbon Story*. I forget what it was about, I forget who was in it, but I still have at the back of my mind its theme tune, which was called "Pedro the Fisherman."

This is because I have always been fond of whistling, and "Pedro the Fisherman" is the quintessential whistling tune—jaunty, catchy, with a touch of the sentimental and an unobliterat-able melody. I like to think that it also expresses the generic character of people who like to whistle, and although I know it can sometimes be intolerable to have an habitual *siffleur* in the family, forever performing "Pedro the Fisherman," still I mourn the decline of the whistlers.

For they are almost a vanished breed these days, and with

them has gone a manner of public thought and conduct. Something *cocky* has left society. The whistling errand boy, the whistling postman, the whistling housewife in her flowered apron, Pedro himself, all were expressing in their often discordant music something at once communal and defiant. On the one hand it was a declaration of liberty, on the other it was a kind of mating call, inviting anybody of like mind to share in its attitudes. By and large, whistlers didn't give a damn, and if whistling was a cock of the snook at respectability, decorum, and frequently musical good taste, it was fundamentally honest. You might be maddened by the sound of it, but at least you knew you could trust a whistler.

I don't know when whistling started, primevally I imagine, but all down the generations the practice has helped to ease the passage of the nations. Think of the marching armies, whistling their way to war! Think of the illicit lovers, whistling home the morning after! Or the errant schoolboys, whistling up their bravado as they make for the headmaster's study! Whistling not only cheers up the whistler; it invites the world at large to cheer up too.

Sometimes the practice of whistling is indeed resuscitated, when a whistle tune is made transiently popular by a movie or a TV ad. But it's never the same. It is whistling, so to speak, to order. It doesn't spring from the public heart. It contains neither the fine careless rapture nor the spirit of independence that comes from random whistlings in the street.

Perhaps it takes either joyous success or optimism in adversity, to set the nations whistling again. We of the twenty-first century are in limbo time, injury time maybe. Popular music has mostly abandoned the melodic line, and when I myself need a shot of the old exhilaration I often return to the end of Pedro's song, which has the fisherman merrily whistling his way to sea with his love in his arms. The tune goes like this—but no, dear friends, I'm afraid you must imagine my lyrical whistle for yourselves.

On Kissing

YEARS AGO MY daughter-in-law, learning that I was just off to California, had a T-shirt printed for me with the slogan NO HUG ZONE. She was aware of Californian proclivity in these matters, and she knew how I felt about unsolicited expressions of indiscriminate affection. I wore the shirt sometimes in America, to minimal effect, but anyway I have since been reconciled to off-the-peg hugging, despite the preposterous antics of footballers (and even cricketers these days, dear God!). At its best, of course, a hug is a generous gesture of friendship, reconciliation, and shared enthusiasm, but even at its worst I see it now as a harmless display of camaraderie, even of common fellowship in the family of man. Long ago it used to be a useful physical device for stabbing an enemy in the back, in the most literal sense. Nowadays even its hypocrisy is mild.

But profligate kissing is a different matter. To my mind a kiss means infinitely more than a hug. I know that many peoples around the world have always used it as a casual form of greeting—in London the quick peck on either cheek used to be the standard onstage identification of a Frenchman—but its adoption in the English-speaking nations has got out of hand. In my opinion it must be curbed. Aesthetically, morally, hygienically, even functionally it has been degraded into the silliest form of social cliché.

Today it is not only the theatrical sort of folk who cry "Darling!" at plush restaurants and assault you with kisses. Everybody does it now. Meet for a coffee at Starbucks, and it starts and ends with kisses. Run into your next-door neighbour at Tesco, and you get a smacker. Hardly have you been introduced to some total stranger, indeed, than you are air-kissed when you part. Mistletoe? Who needs mistletoe!

But in fact those old sprigs of Christmas were a reminder of the marvellous and mysterious heritage of the kiss. It was no mere peck on the cheek, it was history's most notorious moment of betrayal, when the traitor Judas kissed his master Jesus in the garden. A kiss is not something to be given lightly, or even light-heartedly. It has to it the quality of a pledge, together with intimations of destiny. When the clergyman says to the bridegroom, "You may now kiss the bride," he is (or should be) inviting them to remember Judas, and seal their own solemn promise with the very talisman of trust, a kiss.

In high art, too, the symbolical power of the kiss has often expressed itself. *The Kiss*, with a capital *K*, was the title Auguste Rodin gave to his iconic celebration of love's meaning—two people in the ultimate embrace of embraces, physical sex and mental emotion transcendentally united in erotica. Gustav Klimt famously painted *The Kiss*, too, but in his version the lovers had actually become part of the kiss themselves, transformed by its golden sensuality.

But nowadays it's just "Wow! Haven't seen you for simply ages"—and plonk comes the inevitable kiss. It may not even be plonk, indeed, but only one of those trendy near-miss kisses, or maybe one of the lubricious kind that leaves lipstick everywhere, or the careful sort where the two combatants both wear spectacles, or the fastidious sort wary of flu or halitosis.

Whatever kind it is, there is no nobility to it—and of all the human gestures, to my mind, the kiss from the heart, the kiss of conviction, the kiss of true love—of all the signs we humans make to one another, the Kiss, with a capital *K*, is surely the noblest of all. Dumb down your humour, if you like, trivialize your bedroom sex, degrade your religion, infantilize your animals, but give your kisses the grand mystical respect they warrant.

A Plea for Bad Language

IT SEEMS TO me that bad language is not what it was, at least in English. The blasphemous oaths of old have lost their potency, and except in comic books one seldom sees those explosively suggestive rows of asterisks, exclamation marks, and such that used to stand for bowdlerizing.

The blasphemy, of course, means little nowadays. A religious reference used to give a curse or an oath extra authenticity, but nowadays most of us don't for a moment hesitate to take the name of God in vain, and anyway most of the sacred content was long ago elided into the language. How many of us, when we use the grand old expletive "bloody," recall that we are invoking ("by our Lady") the mother of Christ? Not a stage Cockney in a million, brought up on *My Fair Lady*, knows when he utters the compulsory *"Gorblimey"* that he is really challenging God to blind him. When a Welsh-speaker exclaims "*Godacia!*," his equivalent of Damn!, he little realizes he is echoing the old English curse "God ache you!"

But as religious conviction faded, so did the power of the blasphemous idiom. Even in the nineteenth century a British imperial official, submitting a bulletin about one of the remoter possessions, could report without fear of reproval that the country was bloody, and so were the people. When sex began to supplant religion in the public consciousness, its excitements and taboos became more fertile sources of bad language, but now they, too, are weakening. Only a year or two ago I was proud to get away with using, in the pages of an eminent London daily, the word "bugger," one of Churchill's epithets, but today it is edging its way into polite conversation. "Arse" has just about made it already, and in fact sexual idioms are so commonplace these days that their contribution to bad language has lost all meaning. As long ago as the Second World War I learnt that when a sergeant major barked, "Get a fucking move on," he was being more or less convivial: it was only when he omitted the obscenity that he really meant what he said.

By now the F-word has become so commonplace, throughout the English-speaking world, that one does not even notice it. Children use it in the street. Novelists make the most of it. It has become, in the lexicon of scurrility, a word without meaning. And it is in this way, I fear, that the whole repertoire of bad language is losing its true function and its style—the function of shock, the style of effect. "Bugger off!" really meant something when Churchill used it half a century ago: today it is milksop stuff.

Time has overtaken the vocabulary, because it was based upon now unfashionable conceptions—the mystery of religion, the taboos of sex. What we need now, if the tradition is to be revived, is a glossary of bad language based upon contemporary obsessions, and in particular upon the universal influences of the computer—the Grand and Universal Mystery of our time. Already we think far more about the Internet than about the Last Judgement, and one day, I dare say, reality sex will outdate copulation itself.

We need some cyber-swearing, some reality expletives, to reflect these changes. "Blog off!," perhaps, or "Up your USB!," or "What a load of apping, synching, twittering b——ls." And in case some prissy editor bowdlerizes that last word before it gets into print, let me conclude with this one:

On Kindness

MOST POLITICIANS WOULD give their eyes for a dedicated spiritual constituency. Islamic leaders have one, in the mass of their fervent fellow believers. American presidents, if they are sufficiently evangelical, can rely upon that huge body of American Christian fundamentalists who will see him as one of their own. Much of western Europe, though, is now almost impenetrably secular. Few of us go to church or chapel, most of us are probably agnostic if not decidedly atheistic, and the rest are split into infinite sectarian divisibilities of faith.

But potentially uniting us all, as a force of incalculable strength, is the power of kindness. Kindness, it seems to me, is the one abstraction that can guide our conduct while we await the final revelation (if there is one). It does not pretend to know causes, it does not demand explanations, it accepts all that is loftiest in the religions, and everyone knows what it means. It is a homely conception, unlike love, the Christian preference, which has more complex emotional or sexual connotations, and makes impossible demands upon us. It even stands apart from allegory, because it has no deeper meaning than itself. When Shakespeare set out to characterize a despicable villain, he called him bloody, bawdy, remorseless, treacherous and lecherous, but the climax of his invective, his ultimate, absolute adjective of evil, was—"kindless."

I believe kindness to be a vastly potent asset, for anyone who can harness its energies. It is not just that it is non-religious, or inter-religious. It is omni-religious! Everyone understands the meaning of kindness, and all the great faiths pay service to it. We need no theologians to explain it to us. The least literate of tabloid readers knows what it is about.

Most Western politicians dare not venture into the transcendental, because the moment they tread any religious path, they bore to death most of their electors, and antagonize nearly all the others. But in my opinion there is no context in which the idea of kindness could not play a winning role. The kinder the party, the greater its majority would be; the kinder the leader, the more securely in office; the kinder the State, the more stable. Kissing babies has always been a messy and unconvincing duty of electoral candidates: extending the same emotion as a political manifesto, preferably with a more sincere enthusiasm, could sway the opinions of millions.

In short I believe there to be, latent in kindness, a great conceptual weapon only waiting to be brandished: grander than mere religion, far nobler than greed, more convincing than any political creed. One day years ago, sitting with a friend in a bar in Edinburgh, I embarked upon an impassioned spiel concerning the power of the notion, and in my heightened condition told the barmaid that one day there would be a plaque where I sat, commemorating the birth of the Party of Kindness. "Is that so?" she simply said. "And will I fill your glasses in the meantime?" I wish I really could have seized the idea when I was young, and set out to change the world, but it's too late now.

On Getting Old: An Agnostic Sermon

NOT LONG AGO, my sisters and brethren, I heard somebody eminent and elderly discussing the giving of lectures. For him, he said, the worst part of the experience was getting up on the platform in the first place, and I knew exactly what he meant. Oh, the challenge of those brief steep steps into the limelight, the murmurous hands stretched out to help, the stumbling instant of relief when I reach the podium at last, panting a bit, desperately clutching my script and preparing a feeble quip about senility! It really is at those particular moments, those brief moments of display, that I have first felt myself to be getting old.

It is not, I assure you, because of shame. I am not in the least ashamed of advancing old age. I am rather proud of it, and I have thought about it with interest for years. I am a convinced agnostic, untrammelled by religious conviction, and the prospect of death, the destination of age, has always fascinated rather than perturbed me. Forty years ago and more I prepared a gravestone for my beloved Elizabeth and me, on a slab of grey slate which has been waiting ever since among all the jumble under the stairs. Its words provide my first text for this conceptual sermon, and this is what they say, in Welsh and in English:

HERE ARE TWO FRIENDS,
JAN & ELIZABETH MORRIS,
AT THE END OF ONE LIFE

By this I mean first, that whatever happens in life, friendship can see you through it; and second, that you never know, there may be more lives to come. I conceive of those simple lines in the slate, patiently waiting there among the bric-à-brac, as a reassurance for their eventual readers, and as a comradely greeting too.

Nevertheless my fumbling few steps to the lecture stage do offer another sort of message. I am getting old, and they remind me of that fact. I forget names these days. I lose things. I trip a lot. I am easily irritated. I tell the same stories twice. I need the help of the banisters when I go down the stairs, and I can't abide new pronunciations of the English language. One day you will understand.

You will find increasingly frequent reminders, too, that life is finite, at least in its present form. For instance, consider my library, for so long my pride and my delight. Why go on, as I have for so many years, buying and stacking successive editions of the *Times Atlas*: surely in my time there can't be *many* more frontier changes or new-born republics? However necessary I feel it to acquire the latest revisionary research into the imperial administration of British Somaliland, 1922–28, how many of my heirs will care that it is not in the collection I bequeath them? Am I quite sure that I shall go on enjoying *Private Eye* for the rest of its subscription period, or should I cancel the direct debit on my computer now, if I can discover how to do it?

Naturally, by the nature of things, making a will is a definitive memento mori. In my case everything goes to Elizabeth, but if I outlive her it will all be distributed equally among my four children, except only my house with its library in Wales. This I leave to the most active Welsh patriot among my offspring, with the proviso that it be used always for the benefit of Wales. While I know that Twm will loyally accept that one *pro Cambria* condition, what a wretched trick it will be if he finds himself saddled with cracked window frames, leaky drains, or the early traces of dry rot? Bugger Wales, even he might cry—and he certainly doesn't know the protocol for refusing a bequest. But there we are, all I can do for my children, before I go, is clear up the mess as best I can, lovingly thank them, and wish them luck.

(And what about my dear cat Ibsen? Don't mention him. Don't even think about him. He has already Gone Ahead.)

ONE MUST MAKE the most of old age. We can laugh at it, we can be lachrymose about it, we can certainly deplore it, but we must seek the best in it. During the Second World War, when I was young, half the popular songs of the day were about looking forward to a happier future, or being sentimental about the miserable present, and among them I have thought I might find a second text for this homily. Those songs were about bluebirds flying over the white cliffs of Dover (so far as I know a zoologically unprecedented event)—about how there would always be an England (though not necessarily a Wales)—about waiting with Marlene Dietrich tearfully in the lamplight for the return of the Wehrmacht. They were, in short, soppy songs. So in the event I have had to go much further back for my second text: to an earlier war, and to lines that better express the spirit in which I recommend a contemplation of old age—jauntier, to-hell-with-it, up-yours sorts of lines. They were written by the Welsh pacifist George Henry Powell and set to music by his brother Felix in 1915 (the year in which British casualties in the First World War reached half a million). Here they are:

> What's the use of worrying?
> It never was worth while, so
> Pack up your troubles in your old kit-bag,
> And smile, smile, smile!

No matter that six weeks before he was killed, in the last week of the war, the poet Wilfred Owen ironically used that very text for his bitter poem "Smile, smile, smile." It was a fine injunction anyway. I often use it myself to help me through the unkindnesses of old age—and I urge you, my friends, to quote it to yourselves, too, when the time comes. Keep smiling, not sentimentally, not bitterly or in irony, but what we used to think of as cockney-like.

FOR THERE ARE a few advantages in getting old, and to some degree they compensate for the disadvantages. Make the most of them! With luck, never again will you have to stand in a crowded train: somebody is sure to offer you their seat with a sweet smile, and if that smile strikes you as just a *little* patronizing, well, you must just get used to that. You will see it when your car runs out of gas, when you can't find your credit card in the depths of your handbag, when you interminably hesitate before crossing the road, when you offer the bell-boy an insufficient tip (it was perfectly sufficient twenty years ago), or when you forget that it's Angela who's married to poor George now, not Rosemary, which is the father of dear little Christopher, and for that matter which of the whole lot you are talking to (if any).

From most such predicaments you will be rescued with that ever-understanding smile. Accept it gratefully. It is never meant unkindly, and, as for me, I wryly entertain myself in return with my third text, written by T. S. Eliot in 1922:

> O you who turn the wheel and look to windward,
> Consider Phlebas, who was once handsome and tall as you.

For even if we haven't all been as lovely as ancient Phoenicians, we've stayed the course like champions, have we not, and anyway one of the prizes of old age is its release from competition. To hell with Phlebas! To hell with critics! To hell with gossips and jealousies and snide allusions and petty libels! Be honest with yourself—it really no longer matters what people say or think about you. I myself have been all too conscious about posthumous opinions; but I have come to realize that so long as I am not remembered with shame or embarrassment, posterity's views are unimportant—meaningless even, for posterity too is transient and unreliable.

It doesn't matter—that's the thing. To my mind death will be the ultimate freedom. Phlebas the Phoenician was allegorically free anyway, because dead or alive he existed only in Eliot's brain, but we on our way to death have at least achieved a real liberty of our own. Old age is the right to be absolutely ourselves. Laugh, cry, satirize it, my friends, when your time comes—but make the most of it, too!

HERE IS MY fourth text, taken from a Victorian poem (by Henry Newbolt). It is really propagating the upper-class English morality that has long since been reduced to mockery—the ethos of the stiff upper lip—but it seems to me to offer a good enough ideal for an extra-denominational sermon. It concerns a game of cricket, and the last member of a team who can alone rescue his side from defeat. The sun is beginning to go down, there are only a few minutes left to play, and just the one batsman, alone at the pitch, can win, lose, or draw the match. It's not a matter of fame or reward, Newbolt assures us; it is simply a matter of self-respect; and as evening falls we hear a lonely voice from the crowd around the field shouting what I think of as a proud agnostic exhortation, a godless sermon from the mount:

Play up! Play up! And play the game!

We shall never know how he ended the match. He could risk a flamboyant flourish, of victory or defeat, or he could stonewall for a draw. The game has really been played already: it is only the finale that concerns him now, and there is a sort of lesson in his situation for you and me. It is this: Like that cricketer in his last over, forget the strategy that has brought you to your maturity, and concentrate on your final tactics.

The people you love, your children and your Elizabeth, will find their own way home from the pavilion.

THE AGEING PROCESS, of course, has at once bewitched and dismayed poets and philosophers since the dawn of thought. Shakespeare, as usual, capped it all with his seven ages of man, ending with nothingness, but for my purposes I prefer some lines by Thomas Hood. He was good on melancholy in general, and here he is specifically on getting old:

> Thou'lt find they Manhood all too fast
> Soon come, soon gone! and Age at last
>   A sorry *breaking-up*!

I particularly admire the italics of that "breaking-up," because, believe me, there is to the erosion of old age something alien and uncertain, like a foreign language. For me at least, the difficulties of getting up on those lecture platforms are complex: embarrassment plays a part, of course, and physical debilitation, shortage of breath perhaps, the odd pang in the knee, traces of shame and self-mockery; but there is also a cloudy sensation of disbelief and separateness, as though all the kind people giving me a helping hand are not really there at all, but are figures of illusion, unknown to me. Only when we reach the podium, and they release me laughingly to my microphone, notes, and glass of water, then like the ending of a migraine the cloud clears, and I know them, bless their hearts, for who they are.

There is no denying the physical breaking-up. Some people, naturally, break sooner, more completely, and sometimes more acceptingly than others. For years I pretended, to myself and to others, that it was not happening at all. I still try, as a matter of fact. I take my regular breezy walk beside Cardigan Bay at home, and stick resolutely to its self-imposed disciplines, come drizzle or high water. I try to evade the inevitable exchanges with my contemporaries about the inconveniences of age. I dismiss the awful possibilities of Alzheimer's—"well, dear God, don't we all sometimes forget what we've come upstairs for?"—and I make the comic most of my tendency to fall over.

This is nothing new, anyway. I dare say it was accentuated by some minor brain surgery in the 1970s, an experience I have enjoyed dramatizing as a late demonstration of the ancient Inca technique of trepanning; but actually I have been falling about since I was in my thirties, and I have made frequent profess-sional or artistic use of the habit. I much enjoyed, for instance, falling over while jogging at speed along a crowded sidewalk in Los Angeles, and finding myself skidding between the legs of astonished pedestrians in a most exhilarating way. I was touched when, falling over in a New York cab-rank beside Central Park, I woke from a moment's concussion to find a circle of sympathetic faces, some cabmen's, some horses', compassionately observing me. I was entertained when I fell over in Llandudno, the morning after I had appeared on a local television show. I was sitting dra-matically blooded and bandaged in a public first-aid centre, but as they saw me sitting mutilated there, most passers-by merely remarked, "Hey, Jan, great TV last night!" Yes, falling over has often given me useful literary material.

Not so useful lately, though. There came a time when I found myself crossing city streets with exaggerated caution, slower and slower, carefully and more carefully, until one fateful day I discovered that I needed to walk with a stick. A walking-stick—that very symbol or declaration of old age! For a time I persuaded myself that it was merely a swagger stick, something to flourish stylishly: but I know now that it is an essential part of me, something I miss when I leave it in the car, something that is not an encumbrance, but a friend. Not without humour, either, especially when I trip over it trying to get up to that lecture platform.

Still, the day when I first realized I needed a stick, was a day when I needed that exhortation from the cricket ground—Play up! Play up! And play the game! I recommend the text as a pick-me-up, when old age debilitates.

AGNOSTIC THAT I AM, I accept with wonder and gratitude the beauties of religious conviction, and my sixth text comes from the Holy Bible. I have known its words since I was eight years old, when I sang them in the choir of Christ Church, Oxford (though even in my childhood I kept my fingers crossed during our recitations of the Creed). This is Saint Peter's injunction, in the first years of Christianity, to the Christians of Pontus, Galatia, Cappadocia, Asia, and Bithynia:

> Love one another, with a pure heart fervently! See that ye love one another!

Some of the Bithynians and Cappadocians, I suppose, assumed that the Apostle was counselling them about storing up treasures in Heaven. Sceptic that I am, I prefer to interpret his lovely words, to which I have added my own exclamation marks, as purely temporal advice. We can never know the truth about the afterlife, so I see no point in worrying about it; and I believe anyway that sincere adherence to just one essential rule of conduct should be enough to earn us redemption, if the matter unexpectedly arises when we are committed to our graves. Saint Peter called that ultimate essence Love, pure and fervent. I prefer to think of it as Kindness, an all-embracing, omnipotent virtue, encompassing love, compassion, unselfishness, mercy, and all the other values that almost every religion respects, whatever divinities it prefers to honour. I myself require no holy mumbo-jumbos, miracles and exorcisms, angels and ascensions. I simply believe that everything one does in life can be measured against a scale of kindness. While none of us can ever achieve full marks on the scale, and kindness itself must sometimes be weighed in the balance—is it kind ever to be cruel?—yet it seems to me that if there is any ultimate judge out there beyond the Milky Way, we can hardly be faulted if we have done our kindly best.

So soldier on, dear comrades in Kindness, keep smiling, fervently love your loves, play your later years with a straight bat, forget Phlebas and greet old age not as a breaking-up, but as an overture to a new programme, waiting there under the stairs with the rest of the junk.

Post-mortem

WHETHER DEATH IS an absolute or an allegory, more like kindness or more like The Bridge at Ås, for the moment I am unable to say.

To those who believe in an afterlife it has certainly always been allegory, offering varied futuristic interpretations: eternal torment, for example, all flames and remorse, permanent bliss with the Great Almighty riding a sea of cloud and mercy, or simply reunion with the ones we love, in a hitherto unvisited room next door.

To those who tend to think of it as a full stop, on the other hand, death is decidedly absolute. There it is, take it or leave it, draw no conclusions, look for no meanings—think of it, as the Japanese kamikaze commander Admiral Takijiro Onishi wrote in 1945, just before he killed himself, as "a million years of slumber."

For myself, as one who has vastly enjoyed the mortal span, and greatly loved my loves, I hazily suspect that when we die all our essences return unknowing into the fructifying compost of life. I don't much worry about it. I had our tombstone carved thirty years ago, and it's been lying around the house ever since, waiting for its time to come—like most of us, I expect, I think not so much about my own demise as about the happiness of those I shall leave behind. Of course it must be different for people, if there are any still, who believe in the literal existence of hell, and who are convinced that when they die they may be instantly transferred to unremitting torment. That must be seriously worrying—forget your grieving relatives!—but fortunately I cannot conceive of any kind of divine being so sadistic that he would decree perpetual punishment for the kind of miserable sin most of us commit, or any kind of sin for that matter.

Nor have I ever understood the preoccupation of many people, not least Christian people, with the disposal of the body. The fuss they make about funerals! The cost of coffins! Whether or not one believes in the existence of the soul, or worries about an afterlife, surely the wretched corpse itself, no longer even functioning, and never more than a sort of machine anyway, is not worth caring about—throw it away, get rid of it like a rusted freezer, it can't be recycled (well, not all of it, not yet anyway). I don't care what they do with mine, but I have suggested that after removing useful parts they burn it without ceremony, and scatter the ashes on an islet I possess in the river Dwyfor, below my house, where my beloved Elizabeth will, I hope, be similarly distributed.

I have deposited my will with William George and Son, Solicitors/Cyfreithwyr, 103 Stryd Fawr, Porthmadog—

"Incorporating," as they used to say on their letterhead, "Lloyd George and George," Lloyd George being the former Prime Minister of Great Britain, George being his brother who was, when I met him, at 101 the oldest practising solicitor in Britain. As the document in the hands of those gentlemen instructs, a year and a day after Elizabeth and I have both departed, and the grief is over, I would like us to be remembered with a merry wake, down there on the river-bank, with music, champagne for one and all (except those who, like me, would prefer a good white burgundy), and perhaps a roasted sheep.

Naturally our lives have not all been merriment—whose lives ever are? We have had our shares of sorrow. We have squabbled sometimes, although we have never let the sun go down without reconciliation. Elizabeth has had to surmount an obviously less than perfect marriage. I have had to run the gauntlet of those more interested in my gender than in my books. My dear children's troubles, transient or tragic, have been my troubles too. Nevertheless I can selfishly say that, for myself at least, Life has been one long fascination, sprawling, peculiar and generally kind.

Has it been allegory or absolute? Time will presumably tell. In the meantime, after fifty-eight years of intricate friendship (married in 1949, nominally divorced in 1972), on the afternoon of April 14, 2008, Elizabeth and I re-formalized matters in a legal civil union. She thought it a charming but essentially trivial little ceremony, because she considered that we had never been disunited anyway. I viewed it allegorically, of course. I thought it a gesture of high romance. Also I prefer life to be rounded, if not actually symmetrical, and it seemed to me that a final pledge of fidelity before the Dwyfor Registrar would provide a harmonious conclusion to this last attempt at literature.

So with the encouragement of the Morysiad we once again sealed our relationship while the going was good, witnessed by the Rev. and Mrs. Meirion Roberts, formerly of Patagonia, and celebrating the occasion with Earl Grey tea and fruit-cake at Pwllheli.